LOOKING BACK II

MORE TALES OF OLD EAST CONTRA COSTA COUNTY

AN ILLUSTRATED HISTORY

BY

EARL J. HOHLMAYER

MORE THAN THREE HUNDRED PHOTOGRAPHS

First Edition 1996

Published by E & N Hohlmayer
19 West 7th Street
Antioch, Ca., 94509
Telephone (510) 757-8270

ISBN 0-9651251-0-6

Printed in United States by **usprint**
Brentwood, California 94513

DEDICATION

Again this book is dedicated to those men and women who, over the many many, have collected, preserved, copied and orally remembered details of our history. We thank them for the tales of what happened to the early inhabitants, doctors, merchants and others. Also for the stories about the building of East Contra Costa County.

ACKNOWLEDGMENTS

The author wishes to thank the many persons who have contributed to the publishing of this book.

Thanks to Charles Bohakel Jr., fellow historian, for his generous contribution of photos. To Henry Beede for the use of his photo collection.

Thanks to the Henry family for their many photos of Anna Noia Henry and her voyage and thanks to Cathy Miller for the use of the newspaper library. To Valdine Angelo for use of her father's photos.

Thanks to Stamm family for their history of Ferd Stamm. Also my thanks to the Contra Costa History Center and the Antioch History Society.

Thanks to Tom Youell for his grandfather's photos of The "El Primero". And Admiral Jack Garrow for his aid in the Roosevelt Jubilee.

Many thanks to the late Charles B. Weeks Jr., historian, who made the Balfour-Guthrie story outstanding with his memories and generous use of his many photos. This book also is dedicated to Charles' memory.

Thanks to Ida Getz and the many others who have helped with this book.

And last, my thanks to my uncle, Arthur F. Hohlmayer, whose contribution helped publish this book

Cover design by Cynthia Conrad and Author.

TABLE OF CONTENTS

EARLY PITTSBURG (NEW YORK OF THE PACIFIC, BLACK DIAMOND, ETC.)

The Los Medanos Rancho, consisting of two leagues, was granted to brothers, Jose and Antonio Mesa by Mexican Governor Juan B. Alvarado on November 26, 1839. This rancho was to become the site of Pittsburg. Colonel Jonathan D. Stevenson with his partner, Dr. W. C. Parker, bought the property containing 8,890.26 acres from the Mesas in 1849 for the sum of 500 pesos and acquired title on February 24, 1853. He hired two army officers, Maj. R. P. Hammond and Lt. William Tecumseh Sherman, to survey and lay out the site of New York of the Pacific. Each were paid $500 and given 10 or 15 lots of the town site, Sherman said he sold enough of his lots to make another $500. In later years, Sherman became the famous Civil War general.

Stevenson hired the brothers, William Wiggins Smith and Joseph H. Smith, to build the first building, a public house, named the New York House, on his property in 1849. The two men were carpenters and reverends. For their services as carpenters they received $14 a day. The brothers jointly took two quarter sections of land several miles east of New York of the Pacific in July 19, 1849. This would become Antioch.

The Smith Brothers bought the New York House and conducted a temperance eating and boarding house at New York of the Pacific when the town was a flourishing hamlet of 500 souls. The Smiths charged $1 a night for lodging. This was a place on the floor with the person using his own blanket. After working all day, they frequently fried $50 worth of donuts and bread. The bread sold for $1 a loaf. The meals, costing $1, were of beef and bread with, occasionally, fruit and butter. The temperance house was very successful and popular with the river boatmen and travelers.

Another boarding house was the ship, "Mount Vernon" which was converted into lodging by Howard Nichols in 1850.

Stevenson made William Wiggins Smith the first Alcade of New York of the Pacific. The Alcade had charge of all sanitary, civil, criminal and judicial affairs of his district, with full power to appoint his officers, levy taxes and collect fees. Smith spent some $2000 in time, money and medicines in caring for the sick and dead, none of which was ever reimbursed and he found the position was honorary and very expensive. He resigned as Alcade.

The town's name, New York of the Pacific, was dropped in the 1850s and it was named Junction for a short time and then the name New York Landing was chosen.

The little village did not grow until the coal was discovered in 1859 on Mt. Diablo and the mines located at Nortonville, six miles south of town, started shipping coal by horse and wagon (later in 1860 by railroad) to the San Joaquin River. There the coal was loaded on river boats and sent to San Fransisco, Sacramento and Stockton. The town's name was then changed to Black Diamond.

The first post office for the district was located at New York of the Pacific. The town was officially called Junction at that time and the first postmaster was John Beener. In 1852, the Postal Service moved the post office to Antioch.

When the coal mines at Nortonville began to run out of coal, Colonel Stevenson and his partner sold their property. It passed through several owners before it was acquired by San Fransisco banker, Louis A. Pioche, who in turn sold the Los Medanos Rancho to Lester L. Robinson. He was a land speculator, railroad builder and attorney. He built the first railroad in California. It ran from Sacramento to Folsom

When Robinson bought the Rancho he did a lot of improvements to the property. His home was a private estate of 100 acres. He built two windmills which pumped adequate water from the San Joaquin River to water his ranch lands. He built roads, buildings, fences, planted trees and rare plants. Three railroad stations were located on the rancho in 1870...Antioch, Los Medanos and Cornwall. There were three wharves for the steamboats which stopped for passengers and freight. Robinson had a private dock for his ranch.

Robinson lost the Los Medanos Rancho when he got into financial difficulties and the German Loan and Saving Bank of San Fransisco foreclosed after years of litigation. When the bank held an auction for the property in 1900, Charles A. Hooper and his brother, George William Hooper, were the highest bidders and bought the remaining 8,500 acres of the rancho from the bank.

In 1865, C. A. Hooper had started a lumber company in San Fransisco and became quite wealthy. He invested heavily in California land, ranches and timber tracts and owned many lumber companies. Among them was the Sacramento Lumber Co., L. W. Blinn Co., Southern California Lumber Co., Oregon and California Lumber Co. to name a few of his holdings. Mr. C. A. Hooper was a millionaire many times over. He sold one of his lumber companies for $4,000,000.

Hooper was to be a blessing to Pittsburg as he turned the town into a prosperous place with his efforts to bring industry into the area. He was known to be the designer and builder of the city. Hooper was in touch with every business opportunity and while refraining from becoming financially involved with local trade, he was always ready to advise and encourage local movement in a business or social way calculated to benefit the city. Hooper built a country home on part of his property in Pittsburg and spent much of his time there.

In 1900, Black Diamond Street was lined with hotels, saloons, boarding houses and other small businesses. Also, there were many houses and scows of ill-repute in the area. Pittsburg's first bank, the Contra Costa County Bank was organized in 1903 by C. A.

Hooper and his brother, George and began business on January 1, 1904. The capital was $50,000. The second bank was the First National Bank which began business in 1919 with a capital of $100,000.

The Pittsburg Post was established as a weekly paper in 1900 and was the first newspaper to be started in Pittsburg. E. M. Bergthold was the owner.

C. A. Hooper and his brother, George dissolved their partnership in 1906 and the firm then became the C. A. Hooper Company.

Hooper's Redwood Manufacturing Company was Pittsburg's first factory in 1903. He started the first electric power company for the city. The Great Western Power Co. bought his system in 1910. The Bower Rubber Company became the second factory in 1906. In 1910, the first steel mill, Columbia-Geneva Steel began operating with 60 employees.

With the new industries on the rise, a city election in 1911 decided the final name of the city would be Pittsburg.

In 1870, Pietro Aiello, an Italian immigrant, became the town's first fisherman. Four years later in 1874, Pietro and his brother returned to Sicily. Their tales of the great fishing in America on the San Joaquin and Sacramento Rivers started the first of many Italian immigrants on their way to Black Diamond. The first newcomers were from one fishing village in Sicily known as Isola Delle Femmine. Pieto Aiello returned to Pittsburg with a new bride.

Aiello had started the fishing industry that resulted in work for hundreds of people in fishing and in the fish canneries of the town. The fishermen from Greece had heard about the marvelous fishing and also made the town their home. Black Diamond was populated with a great many Greeks and Italians.

One of the first canneries was the Pioneer Cannery and another was the Black Diamond Cannery. The F.

E. Booth Cannery was built in 1917 and became one of largest sardine canneries in the world at that time. It was built at the foot of Cumberland Street on the old site of the Sacramento River Packer's Association cannery that was established in 1903 and acquired by Booth. Frank Booth, his father and a partner named Storey owned a cannery at Collinsville before he built the new cannery at Pittsburg. Other canneries were Paladini, Standard Fisheries, Limberg Salmon Packers and Western California. The canneries biggest items shipped were salmon, sardines and shad. The canneries also processed and shipped fruits and vegetables. They processed barrels of salted salmon that were shipped as far away as Germany. Fresh fish (shad, salmon and catfish) packed in ice were sent to San Fransisco, Los Angeles and as far away as Denver and Philadelphia. Ocean going vessels docked at the canneries on the waterfront, picking up their loads of canned fish.

Hundreds of Italian and Greek fishermen worked the rivers and bays for nine months out of the year. The Italians would take their young sons out of school to help with the fishing. They said 8th grade was long enough education for their sons. After two years fishing experience, they were allowed to operate their own boat.

The vessels used by the fishermen were many fallucas, an Italian single-masted boat, gill-net smacks and the double-ended gasoline powered boats, which was later known as the "Monterey". This sturdy boat was powered with a one cylinder Hicks gasoline engine. Many of these Montereys are still in existence and are a prized procession of boat collectors.

Because the fishing season extended for months, the men towed houseboats with their vessels to the fishing locations. During that time they lived aboard the houseboat.

In 1889, within a radius of ten miles of Pittsburg and Antioch, 120 boats with 350 Italian and Greek fish-ermen caught an average of 3000 salmon and sturgeon fish daily. Their fishing season that year was nine months.

When the local fishing season ended, many of the fishermen made the trip to Alaska on sailing vessels for the Alaskan salmon fishing season. They were paid 3 cents per fish and usually earned a total of $200 for their Alaskan fishing season

With all the fishermen working in the area, another industry needed was the boat-building industry. This was first filled by Frank Seeno in 1892. He designed and built the double-ended gasoline powered fishing boat. It had a retractable keel so it could be maneuvered in shallow waters and the rudder was removable to be able to bring gill-nets up over the stern. This boat gradually replaced the sail boats and became very popular with all fishermen in California and was known as the "Monterey". These motor equipped boats made the fisherman's life easier and they could return home each night after fishing. Seeno's boatyard was in existence for many years. Other boat builders were the Del Montes and Frank Cardinalli

The Johnson and Lanteri Shipyard was established in 1909 and was Pittsburg's biggest yard, located on the waterfront near the Columbia Steel Company. They built many dredgers, two which were the largest dredgers ever built in the world. Dredgers were in great demand for use in the Delta and the shipyard was ideally located for the building of these vessels. The shipyard also built ferry-boats, tow-boats and other types of vessels.

Charles Hooper was involved in the organization of Columbia Steel Company as he was an associate of the Charles M. Gunn Associates who were in charge of building the foundry. He owned real estate along the river and was instrumental in getting Pittsburg the location for the foundry. In November 1910, the businessmen watched as the first heat of steel was tapped and poured from the single 15-ton open hearth. The plant began on 20 acres of land and Charles M. Gunn was the company's first president. The close proximity of the Columbia Steel Company provided much of the steel castings needed by the Johnson and Lanteri Shipyard. The mill produced steel casting for use in ships, dredges and lumber companies. One article in the Antioch Ledger said..."What is claimed to have been the largest casting ever produced in any foundry west of Chicago was poured at the Columbia Steel Company's foundry at Pittsburg. The casting is for the battleship "Montana" and will weigh thirty tons when dressed to proper size. It will require two weeks time for the huge mass of steel to cool". Columbia Steel Company was bought by United States Steel Corporation in 1929.

The Great Western Electo-Chemical Company was established in Pittsburg on February 1916. The chemical company was located east of the Columbia Steel Co. by the old coal mine railroad dock. They manufactured caustic soda, liquid chlorine, aqua ammonia and other chemicals used in many products and processes of production. In 1936 the company merged with the Dow Chemical Company of Midland, Michigan and became the western division of Dow.

Another chemical company located in Pittsburg was the Shell Chemical Company in 1930, who made ammonia from natural gas that was piped 300 miles from the Buttonwillow oil field. The ammonia could be used as fertilizer, refrigerator refrigerant, household use, and in the manufacturing of explosives. Another company near the city was the General Chemical Company.

Johns-Manville Products Corporation arrived in Pittsburg in 1925. The plant is built on a 25-acre tract in the eastern part of the city on the corner of E. 3rd and Harbor Streets. At that time the company manufactured roofing felt and asphalt

rooting shingles. Employees numbered approximately 200 men.

There were many other factories and businesses located in and near Pittsburg in those early days.

Charles A. Hooper, the designer and benefactor of Pittsburg died at his country home at Pittsburg in 1914. He was 71 years old. The C. A. Hooper Company continued doing successful business in Pittsburg for many years by his heirs and competent managers.

The Los Medanos Hotel was built in 1917 by the C. A. Hooper Company. It was an opulent edifice complete with a lavish restaurant, bar and dance floor. The rooms were equipped with every modern connivance except baths. Only the suites had baths. It's cost was $60,000 and covered one city block on Cumberland Street between 8th and 9th Streets. It was the popular place to have parties and for lodging. unfortunately the hotel was burned to the ground in 1980.

Lodges, churches, schools and libraries were intricately a part of Pittsburg's social life in those days. Pittsburg's little red school house was built in the heart of the business district when the town was New York Landing. It was built of red brick in 1875 and was the second school building with 39 children attending classes. The first school building was a wooden building brought down on a railroad flat car from Nortonville. It was only used as a school for a short time as it soon became inadequate and the much larger brick building was erected.

Masonic Lodge No.249 Pittsburg was organized January 20, 1912 with 22 Master Masons as charter members, most of whom demitted from the Antioch Lodge No.175. I.O.O.F Pittsburg Lodge No.436 initiated 1914. Los Medanos Rebekah Lodge No. 116 Pittsburg was instituted October 12, 1897. Knights of Pythias Black Diamond Lodge No.29 was organized October 1874 with 30 charter members. Native Sons of the Golden West Diamond Parlor No. 246

Pittsburg organized with 27 members on February 4, 1909. Also the Native Daughters of the Golden West Stirling Parlor No. 146 Pittsburg.

At first, Catholic Mass was held in homes and the marriages and baptisms were performed in the Catholic church in Antioch. In 1900, the first Catholic church, Saint Peter Martyr's, was built at the corner of Cutter and Second Streets. It burned down in 1906. Another church building was erected and blessed there in 1910. It had a belfry which the Fire Department used to sound the fire alarm, This church was moved on rollers pulled by a capstan turned by a donkey to the new location at Black Diamond and Eighth Streets.

Protestant churches were also in Pittsburg in those early days. The first of those were the Congregational and Baptist Churches.

Charles Hooper donated many of the building lots for the communities' churches in the area.

The lodges and churches provided much of the entertainment with dances, festivals (St. Peter's Day for one), picnics and parties. Weddings in the Italian community were always festive occasions.

A Pittsburg tradition was started in 1914 with the Columbus Day Celebration on October 11 and 12. This became a yearly affair and known throughout the State. The Pittsburg Post on October 17 had this to say..." LANDING OF COLUMBUS AT PITTSBURG CELEBRATION...The four hundred and twenty-second anniversary of the discovery of America was fittingly observed in Pittsburg last Sunday and Monday. Excursion trains brought hundreds of visitors from every direction and as a result the principal streets of the city were literally packed with humanity.

The landing of Columbus at 10 o'clock Sunday morning was attended by befitting surroundings (Boat was decked-out to resemble one of Columbus's vessel) with the exceptions of the modern city and it's people which welcomed the illustrious explorer, and the presence of Campell's Amalgamation of shows, the like of which was not known in Christopher's time. But the landing was successful in every particular, and was followed by a well-formed line of floats, headed by the Pittsburg Band which paraded the principal streets.

Conspicuously mounted on towering thrones were the King and Qween, the vehicle being drawn by four prancing steeds. Next came in order the Goddess of Liberty, Christopher Columbus and party, hundreds of school children, the Native Sons Drum Corps of 17 pieces under command of Miss Rhonda Mora and citizens in autos. In the latter division was noted a string of seven new Studebaker cars, 1915 model, placed on exhibition by Casper Cautiello, the enterprising local agent for the Studerbaker Company.

At 12 o'clock interesting speeches were made at the grandstand at West Third and Black Diamond Street by distinguished orators. In the afternoon a variety of sports was offered, affording ample entertainment for all.

Several of the side streets were occupied by carnival companies which offered a varied list of attractions in the way of amusement.

The celebration was pronounced a success in nearly every angle of vision, nothing occurring to mar the pleasure of visitors, nor to cause embarrassment to the Committee in charge of the big event." (end of story)

In the first Celebration, Columbus was impersonated by Anline Geraldo of Antioch, the Queen was Jennie Di Vencenzi of Collinsville and the King was Salvatore Davi of Pittsburg.

This is small part of the early history of Pittsburg.

5

TOWN OF BLACK DIANOMD IN EARLY DAYS DRAWN BY AN ARTIST

6

Pittsburg fishermen towing living quarters to fishing grounds.

Ship loading canned salmon at Pittsburg Waterfront

Famous Monterey fishing boat designed and built
by Frank Seeno of Pittsburg. Cannery in background

FISHERMEN HAVE BOATS BUILT HERE

For Monterey Bay and the Nearby Rivers Trade

TWO LAUNCHED THIS WEEK

G. E. and Frank Seeno Have Monoply in This Line

A visit to the boat building establishment of G. E. Seeno, and to that of Frank Seeno, brother of the former, on Wednesday, by a representative of the Dispatch, disclosed the fact that many fishing boats for the Monterey Bay and Sacramento and San Joaquin rivers trade are being built here in Pittsburg.

G. E. Seeno has most of the work for the Monterey fishermen. He has just completed two handsome fishing boats. One, the "Balbo," the property of Tuirddo Cardinelli, was christened the first of the week and left at once for Monterey.

The other completed boat, which will leave for San Francisco within the next few days, is the property of S. Ciancinnio, and is to enter the crab-fishing trade in San Francisco Bay.

Another fine boat, which is in midway of construction, will go to Monterey when completed, as the property of Giuseppe Bellavista.

Two other boats are in the first stage of construction by G. E. Seeno,

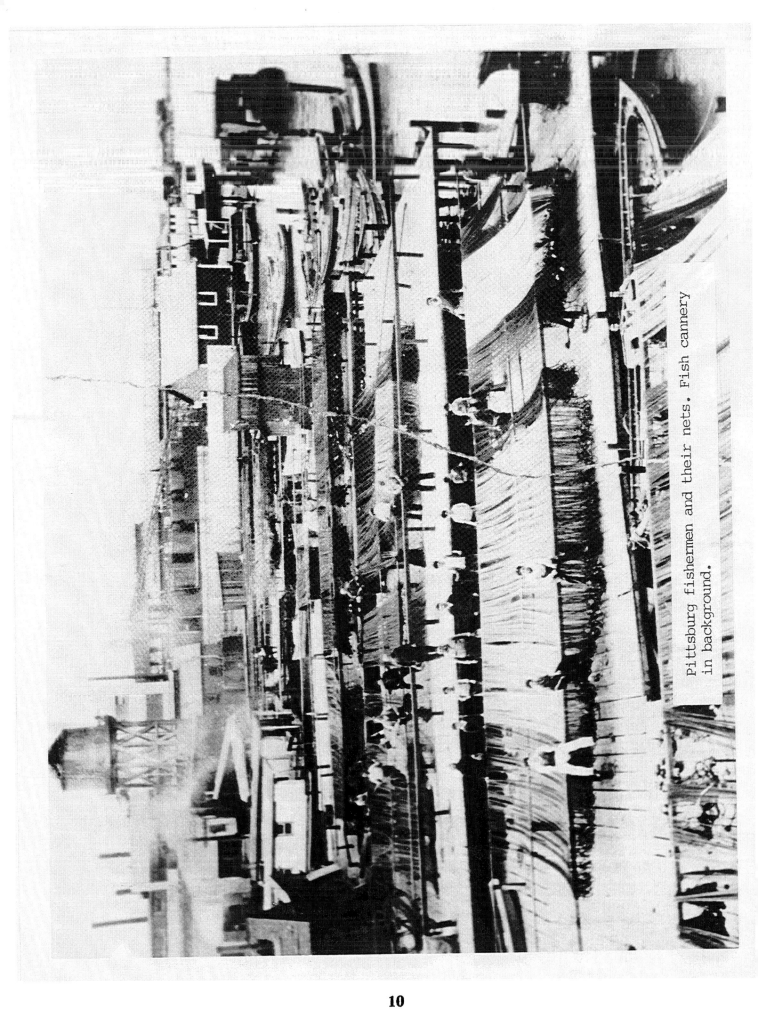

Pittsburg fishermen and their nets. Fish cannery in background.

Columbia Steel ware house.

Columbia Steel Company rolling mill.

Steel mill's engine and cars with scrap iron.

12

Contra Costa Bank and Post Office building.

C. A. Hooper's office of Rancho Los Medanos.

End of Black Diamond Street. Bay View Saloon was the favorite stop for famous author, Jack London, when visiting Pittsburg.

Black Diamond St. looking north from Second St.

Keller's Pharmacy.

Railroad Ave. North from Fourth St.

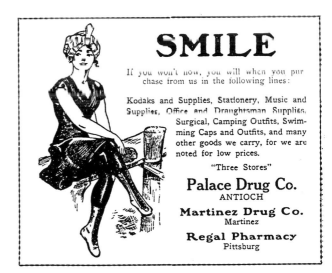
Andrew Daley "Mayor of Cornwall".

Daley's Saloon at Cornwall.

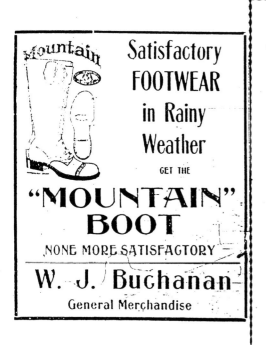

Store and home of County Supervisor W. J. Buchannan. S. W. corner
Second and Black Diamond Streets.

19

Pittsburg Tennis Club, located on S. E. corner of Los Medanos and Fifth Streets.

City pound in 1912 on Railroad Ave.

Santa Fe Railroad Station at Pittsburg

Southern Pacific Railroad Station

21

First school, S. W. corner Cumberland and Fourth Streets.
Building brought down from Nortonville on railroad flatcar.

"The Red Brick School". Second school house

Fairmont Hotel. Black Diamond St. by 2nd St.

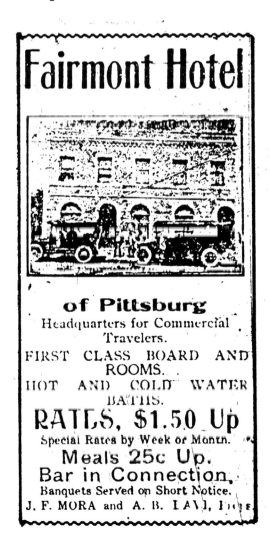
23

Town Jail on 2nd St. between Railroad Ave. and Cumberland St.

Fire House and Town Hall.

Advertise in the Pittsburg Post

WE
GUARANTEE
THAT ALL
JOB
PRINTING
Turned Out of the Office of
THE
PITTSBURG
POST
Will Give Entire Satisfaction

Pittsburg Post Newpaper office.

25

Cappacciotti children, all twelve of them.

Dr. George, Chairman of town's Board of Trustees 1908-1916.

Many Visit the New Hotel

Many of Pittsburg's visitors who were out for a stroll Sunday wended their way toward the new big Hotel Los Medanos, which is nearing comletion, with the object of inspecting the interio of the structor.

All were destined to disappointment, as a watchman was stationed on the grounds, who refused admittance to all who tried to get in.

It is said the hotel will be ready for occupancy about the first of April.

Hotel Los Medanos built in 1917.

Old fire house on Cumberland St. near 4th St.

Residence of Casper Cautiello and the Viscuso Hardware Store.

28

Pittsburg Newspaper advertisements from 1913–1916

Pittsburg Newspaper advertisements from 1913–1916

MT. DIABLO COAL FIELDS

There is some question as to when coal was found in the foot hills of Mt. Diablo. Dr. John Marsh in 1837 wrote to the New Orleans Picayune that there was coal in the foot hills. Coal was discovered in the northeast Mt. Diablo foot hills in 1855 by George W. Hawxhurst and his discovery became the Union Mine. Francis Somers found an out-cropping of coal in the hills east of Mt. Diablo while out hunting game in 1859. This location at the top of Kirker Pass became Nortonville named after Norah Norton who was the first to build a house there and the mines were known as the Black Diamond claim.

The principal mines were the Black Diamond, Cumberland and Mount Hope. All the mines were eventually bought out by the Black Diamond Company and they became the largest operation in the coal fields

Somers and Hawxhurst found a vein of coal in Markley Canyon with five companies eventually operating there. The mining town was named Somersville for Francis Somers. The mining companies were Pittsburg, Manhatten, Union, Eureka and Independent. The Pittsburg Company was the largest and only the Black Diamond Company produced more coal then Pittsburg.

Coal was found by W. B. Stewart, T. K. Shattuck and William Hillegas in 1861 in the Lone Tree Valley. Three towns were founded, Stewartsville, Judsonville and West Hartley.

The many of the veins of coal were located by gold miners who were discouraged in the gold fields and turned to looking for the "black gold". Among the prospectors were Roundtree, William C. Israel, S. B. Whipple, Walker, Dickson and J. T. Cruiksbank who all discovered coal in the Mt. Diablo foot hills. Israel found coal in Horse Haven six miles south of Antioch in 1859.

Coal mines were operated as far east as Marsh's Meganos Rancho, where the Mt. Diablo coal field ended with the Brentwood Mines.

The coal miners were Welsh, Irish, and Italian immigrants and Americans from the coal fields in the eastern parts of the United States.

Nortonville was the largest town of all the coal communities. In the mid-1870s, it was the largest town in Contra costa County with a population of over 1,000 with 300 men and boys working the mines. It had become apparent by 1862 that there was plenty of coal and the mines would be in operation for many years. The miners bought their families to the area and the towns had hotels, bars, saloons, churches, stores, boarding houses post offices and cemeteries. A school was built in 1866 and the miners donated 1% of their pay to finance it. The towns had many fraternal societies. There was also rowdy entertainment and other activities provided by the saloon girls.

The Antioch Ledger in 1870 had this story..."Ferry Boat Detained...Not being favored with sight of Captain Turner and the mail bag at the usual time on Thursday evening, we proceeded to the wharf to ascertain the cause, and found the delay was caused in consequence of the Captain having to transship from the steamer "Chrysopolis" the entire paraphernalia of a Sacramento beer cellar..... piano, waiter-girls, and of those last named there were four, who were neither decorous in behavior nor choice in their language, as they neared our wharf. They are enroute for Nortonville, but previous to their departure gave some specimens of their talent, in the musical line, which culminated in a rough and tumble fight, in which the "fightist" of the crowd was roughly handled. We congratulate our citizens on being spared the infliction...and we cannot rejoice with Nortonville at this accession to their population."

Three railroads were serving the coal mines. These were the first railroads built in Contra Costa County.

At first the coal was hauled from the mines to the ship docks on the San Joaquin River by wagons drawn by six horses or mules. It was possible to haul 10 tons a day by this method in dry weather but during the rainy season six tons of coal a day was considered lucky. Most of the time in the really bad weather the wagons would get bogged in mud. Chase and Robbins Livery Stable in Antioch furnished 40 mules and horses to haul the coal from Stewartsville to Antioch in 1870. During the winter, drayage ceased because of the mired road. Black Diamond Company made the first improvement when they built a wood rail tram road from the mines to New York Landing. (later called Black Diamond, and now Pittsburg). Mules pulled the coal cars to the river docks.

The expensive drayage of the coal from the mines to the river docks by horses or mules and wagons was the reason railroads were built from the three coal regions. In 1866, the first railroad was built. This was the Pittsburg Mine and Railroad Company connecting the Somersville mines in Markley Canyon to Pittsburg Landing. (near the Dow Chemical Plant). The Black Diamond Railroad was completed in 1867. This railroad ran from Nortonville at the head of Kirker Pass to New York Landing (Pittsburg). Before schools were establish in New York Landing, the school children rode the train to the Nortonville school. Charles Mortimer Belshaw and Edward Judson formed the Belshaw Company and bought the Empire Mine and later the Central Mine in the Lone Tree Valley coal field. In 1877, they built their railroad from Stewartsville to the Antioch waterfront, a distance of eight miles. They had to build 11 bridges and a 1000 foot tunnel.

Their company was officially named the Empire Coal Mine and Railroad. The engineer was paid $120 a month and the brake men and firemen drew $50 a month and all the coal and water the railroad crew could use at home.

The Pittsburg and Black Diamond railroads were 5 ½ miles long and had standard gauge rails but the Empire rails were narrow gauge, three feet

wide. All three railroads were built on a grade from the river to the mines of two to five percent. The level of the tracks became five percent steep (350 to 850 foot above river level) as they climbed through the canyons to the mines. Trestles and tunnels had to be built because of the rugged terrain. The level of the tracks allowed the loaded coal cars to coast down to the docks from the mines without the use of the engine. During the wet winter months the tracks were sanded to aid slowing cars by brakes. After the coal was unloaded, the engine pulled the train of cars back to the mines. The school children coming home to New York Landing rode down the tracks in an empty car. They thought it was exciting and exhilarating.

Mr. Belshaw, owner of the Empire Railroad, enjoyed this method of returning back to Antioch. He would ride the train's caboose to Stewartsville, conduct his business there and then have the caboose detached, climb aboard and turn it loose, letting the momentum speed it back to Antioch. People said it was a great sight with him standing at the brake wheel, his hair and coat-tails flying, as the caboose sped down the tracks to Antioch.

Taking the coal out of the mines was fairly easy as the coal was soft and blasting was unnecessary. Accidents caused by gas explosions, fires and falling rock were few but did happen. On July 24, 1876, a fire broke out in one of the Nortonville mines. Six bodies and eight mortally wounded men were brought up from the mine shaft.

After access from the surface was completed, gangways driven on coal seams and with ventilation installed, the mining could proceed. Pumps were also installed as water in the mines was a problem. The type of mining used in these coal fields was called the room and pillar method. The mining teams were an experienced miner and an assistant called a nobber. These assistants were usually boys, some as young as eight years old. The soft lignite coal could be worked loose with a small pick while the miner was kneeling or lying on his side in a space 18 to 54 inches. As the miner worked the coal loose, the nobber would load it on a steel lined wooden chute and slide it down to the gangway. It was then loaded on one to one and half ton capacity cars that were brought to the surface by horse, mule or manpower. Working ten to twelve hours a day by candle-light or oil lamp, six to seven days a week, the team was paid from 75 cents to a dollar per cubic yard of coal.

When the coal arrived on the surface it was transferred to the bunkers located at the town sites where it was screened into commercial sizes known as lump and small coal. Some of these bunkers held as much as 1,800 tons of coal. Trains were then loaded and sent to the river docks where the river boats were loaded. The coal was then transported to San Fransisco, Stockton and Sacramento. Black Diamond Company had their own boats to transport the product to the markets which gave them an edge over the other coal mine companies.

The local coal industry declined because of increased costs, the discovery of higher quality coal in Washington and Oregon States and the use of oil as a power source. In an attempt to lower labor costs, Chinese laborers were brought in but this resulted in strikes and labor unrest. The mines closed during 1885 to 1902. Black Diamond Company ceased operations in 1885 and moved their equipment to the Washington coal fields. Pittsburg Mine closed in 1902. The Empire Coal Mines and Railroad Company was sold by Senator Belshaw in 1902 and the property was dismantled.

A value of 14,500,000 dollars of coal was mined from the Mt. Diablo coal fields. This is priced at the dollar value of the era. In the first year of practical operation 200,000 tons of coal was mined. The last year

of mining in 1902 the tonnage was 13,960.

Oil was discovered in the Mt. Diablo coal fields in 1864. The discovery of oil fields in California helped lead to the closure of the coal mines in the Mt. Diablo coal fields. The import of lower cost foreign coal and the lower cost of oil and gas as a power source doomed the local mines.

Silica sand was discovered at the Somersville and Nortonville sites in 1922. It was used by glass companies to manufacture glass and used at the Columbia Steel mill to make sand casting molds for their steel products. It was mined until 1949.

The sites of the old mines are now part of the Black Diamond Regional Preserve of the East Bay Regional Park District.

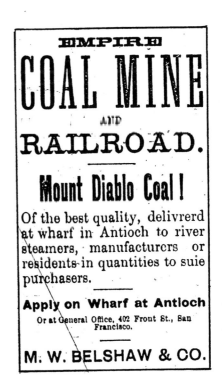

Stewartville townspeople near the Central mine
coal bunker in 1882.

Side view of Central Mine coal bunker. Stewartville.

All mine photographs, unless specified, are from Charles Bohakal Jr. Collection

Empire Mine Railroad crew, left to right, Bill Bullock-
fireman, Elmer Page-brakeman, S.K.McKellip-engineer and
Putman Reed-brakeman. From the J.E.Boynton Collection

Empire Railroad train on one of the trestles.
From the J.E.Boynton Collection

Empire Railroad train at the unloading dock in Antioch.
From the J.E.Boynton Collection

Nortonville Main Street in 1878

School Hill looking west in the 1870s, Nortonville

Black Diamond coal train.

General store and Post Office at Sommersville.
From Author's Collection

Nortonville Grammar School in the 1870s. Children from the town of Black Diamond were brought by the coal train to this school.

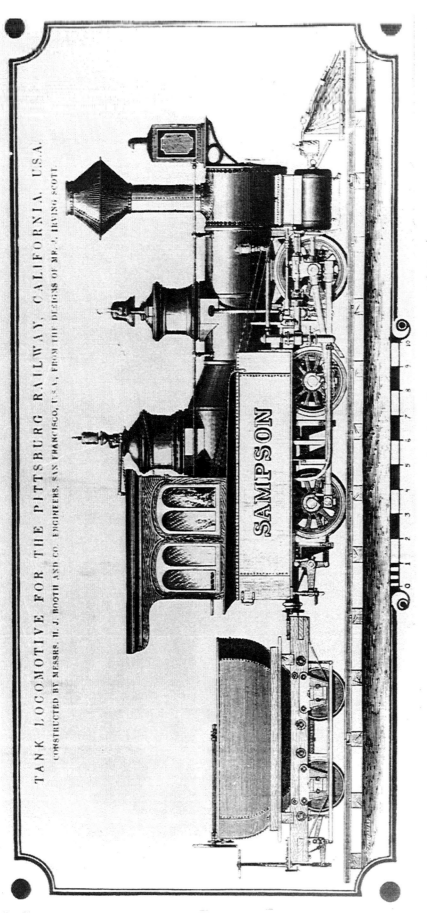

TANK LOCOMOTIVE FOR THE PITTSBURG RAILWAY, CALIFORNIA, U.S.A.

CONSTRUCTED BY MESSRS. H. J. BOOTH AND CO. ENGINEERS, SAN FRANCISCO, U.S.A., FROM THE DESIGNS OF MR. J. IRVING SCOTT

SAMPSON

Drawing of the Pittsburg Coal Mine Company locomotive.

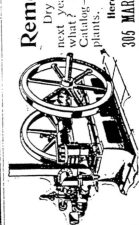

A new landmark era in the history of East Contra Costa County was the coming of the San Pablo & Tulare Railroad which was a branch line of the Central Pacific System. This railroad later became the Southern Pacific Railroad.

Until 1877, the only means of transportation between Stockton, Antioch, Pittsburg and other towns to the outside world were the riverboats and the stage lines.

About this time the Central Pacific began to consider building a railroad to tap the resources of the country between San Fransisco and Stockton. In this era, Antioch was the center of a great grain growing area and many shiploads of wheat, barley and other grains were shipped out from Antioch's wharves.

It seemed that the ideal rail line should run through Antioch along the river front. Had that happened, the huge grain warehouses which made Port Costa a great shipping center would have been located in Antioch.

This came very close to fruition when prominent Antioch residents and Friedlander, the "Grain King" of that era, convinced railroad officials to run the route along the water front through Antioch. Their one provision was that ships of 21 feet draft could be loaded at the local wharves. Local business men and financiers raised a fund and General S. B. Alexander of the U. S. Army conducted a survey of the water front and the water depth. His report was favorable and the town's hopes were high but the railroad, however, chose not to build on that route.

Reports at the time said that the Southern Pacific was built on it's present right-of-way because of the high price of waterfront property. This was refuted by Henry F. Beede, then an 18 year-old office clerk for Joseph Galloway, principal owner of the Antioch Lumber Company, the waterfront and much of the townsite. Young Beede reported at a meeting of the railroad director and the townspeople

that the right-of-way would have been donated outright to the railroad company.

Following Alexander's report, several officials of the Central Railroad System, including president Leland Stanford, Charles Crocker, A. N. Towne and Arthur Brown, came to Antioch on a special steamer and met with townspeople in Galloway's lumber company office. Beede was present at the interview and said the railroad officials were offered every inducement to build the road through the town and along the waterfront. And, though the meeting was deemed successful, no official decision was made.

The arrogant attitude of the railroad was evident by a remark made by Charles Crocker at that meeting. He said... "Railroads are to a certain extent, of course, servants of the people; but when it comes to building and developing towns, the railroad usually prefers to build it's own towns."

Shortly after this meeting, "Grain King" Friedlander, who had pushed for the waterfront railroad line in Antioch, Dropped dead on the streets of San Fransisco and the grain situation was temporarily demoralized. In the meantime, the San Pablo & Tulare Railroad decided on it's present route several miles south of Antioch. The officials probably thought the town would move to the railroad station but it didn't for a number of years. For a long time there was only a saloon and the station at that location.

After difficulties in securing right-of-ways (which was instrumental in securing the passage of "Eminent Domain" laws.), the railroad was completed and until 1888 was the only railroad in Contra Costa County.

A second railroad finally arrived in Antioch July 1, 1900. The making of the line began in 1895 with the efforts of San Fransisco merchants and local residents who pushed for another railroad to compete with the Southern Pacific (formerly the S P & T Railroad). The San Fransiscans raised $2.5 million dollars, and on Feb 25, 1095, the articles of incorporation of the San Fransisco and San Joaquin Valley Railroad was filed. The line was to go from San Fransisco through Stockton to Bakersfield.

A Nov 20, 1897 article in the Daily Ledger reported on the survey across the tules from Stockton toward Antioch that was recently completed. The survey showed the distance from Stockton to Antioch was 22 miles. The only question unanswered was the location of the line through Antioch. According to the Salt Lake Survey it would run through the southern suburbs of the city on Eight Street immediately south of the old Catholic church. The editor of the Ledger, however, wrote that the proper route should run to the north of town along the riverfront. He said it was of vital importance the road be built there, pointing out that the river was the primary reason for the development of the town and the utilization of it by the railroad was the future of Antioch.

In addition, the townspeople and merchants wanted the passengers to see the water and shipping after traveling through southern deserts and arid plains. They felt it would create a very favorable opinion and a lasting impression of Antioch. The following is part of the Nov 20, 1897 editorial.-.."The road should run down First Street and the town should see that it had free right-of-way. Any property owner who is stingy and mean enough to stand in the way as an obstructionist, should be dumped in the river. The man who shows the cloven hoof in this respect will be the enemy to the town and should be executed.

The warehouse owners, the lumber company and coal road might be slightly inconvenienced, but we do not believe they will interpose any stumbling block. They have, in many instances, been granted many privileges by the town and it would certainly show a dog-in-the-manger spirit to stand in the way now that the town has an opportunity. The town trustees should

meet and canvass the situation and be in a position to offer the right-of-way down the waterfront.

And our prominent citizens should combine and divert proper influence to induce the railroad to take this route through town. The opportunity has arrived and it now only remains to be seen whether our citizens are equal to the opportunity."

In a later Ledger article a head surveyor of the Valley Railroad reported that the route would be along the waterfront. The Antioch Lumber Company had given right-of-way through it's property, and since the company owned most of the waterfront, there was no opposition from others.

In the same issue of the Ledger, another article said the site for the depot had not been selected and prospective owners were warned not to jeopardize the interests of the town by refusing to sell their property at a fair value to the company. The railroad bought property on the north-west corner of Main (now I Street) and First Streets and decided to build a new depot instead of remodeling the old Homburg Hall that was standing there. (This "new" Santa Fe depot was destroyed by arsonists in 1984).

The building of the road progressed rapidly and by June 24, 1899, the contractors were rushing the work. The trestle across the water near the Antioch distillery was almost ready for track laying. The trestle for the Empire Coal Railroad at the end of F street was finished and the Empire Railroad was back in business of shipping coal. the steamer "Sunol" delivered 11,000 railroad ties to the lumber wharf. About 2,000 tons of steel rails were about to be brought to Antioch and stored at the Railroad storage yards east of Antioch.

The high bank was removed by the hay warehouses at the end of G Street and widened enough to put in a spur to the warehouses.

The sand dunes were leveled east of Antioch and the sand was used to ballast the rails and for fill. The marsh-sinks by the Steamboat Wharf, Antioch and Pittsburg Landings were filled using the excess sand.

Track laying began in August 1899. At this time, President E. P. Ripley of the Santa Fe Road was elected president of the San Fransisco and San Joaquin Valley Railroad. It wasn't long until it was absorbed by the Santa Fe Railroad.

By October, 1,500 carloads of dirt was added to the sand already placed in the sink by the old Steamboat Wharf and it was ready for the tracks. By July 1, 1900, all the tracks were laid and the first passenger train arrived in Antioch from Stockton. the train, which was filled with railroad officials, included an engine and tender, baggage car, and a buffet car. It was met by a crowd that gathered along the track to welcome the first passenger train into Antioch over the Valley Road.

The Ledger said..."A short stop was made and the engine took on some water, so the first train into Antioch left some money in town for they are buying water from Mr. Belshaw."

The new road got the lion's share of Antioch's business by running it's route along the waterfront. Approximately 8,000 carloads a year of various products were shipped in the 1900s. Antioch was the asparagus capital of the world and this product, along with celery, peaches, pears and other green fruits were shipped by the Santa Fe Refrigerator Dispatch trains to eastern cities. One month the receipts for freight charters at the Santa Fe office was $150,000. The revenue for the passenger business ranged from $3000 to $5000 a month.

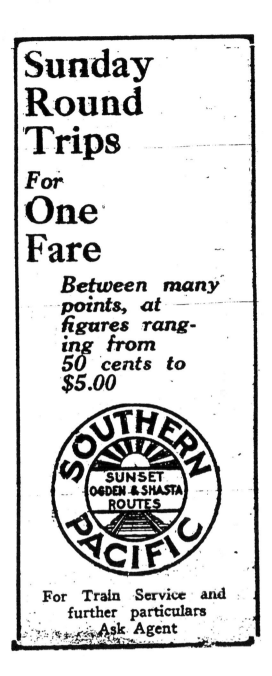

TIME TABLE
SOUTHERN PACIFIC R. R.
TO SAN FRANCISCO

Train	Arrive
No. 57	5:38 a.m.
No. 49	11:50 a.m.
No. 55	4:28 p.m.
No. 35	8.55 p.m.

TO TRACY AND LOS ANGELES

Train	Arrive
No. 36	8:05 a.m.
No. 56	1:53 p.m.
No. 50	6:00 p.m.
No. 58	1:53 a.m.

SANTA FE TIME TABLE
EFFECTIVE NOVEMBER 14.
Arrival and departure of trains.

Train	Arrive
	FROM SAN FRANCISCO
No. 10	10:26 a.m.
No. 22	1:23 p.m.
No. 42	7:14 p.m.
No. 2	12:37 a.m.
	FROM STOCKTON
Train	Arrive
No. 21	5:45 a.m.
No. 11	11:05 a.m.
No. 9	6:33 p.m.
No. 5	8:10 p.m.

SOUTHERN PACIFIC DEPOT AND MDSE. DEPOT

Southern Pacific freight train at S.P.Depot at Railroad and A Streets.
Courtesy Charles Bohakel Jr. Collection

44

Santa Fe workers, telegrapher and station manager at Antioch Depot.
Courtesy Charles Bohakel Jr. Collection

Santa Fe steam engine and freight car.
Courtesy Charles Bohakel Jr. Collection

Early freight train in East Contra Costa County.
Courtesy Charles Bohakel Jr. Collection

Santa Fe steam engines. Courtesy Charles Bohakel Collection

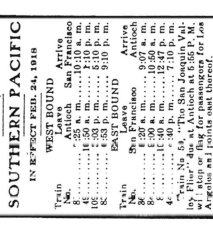

47

Passingers waiting for train at Antioch Santa Fe Station. 1904

SANTA FE R. R. DEPOT, ANTIOCH, CAL.

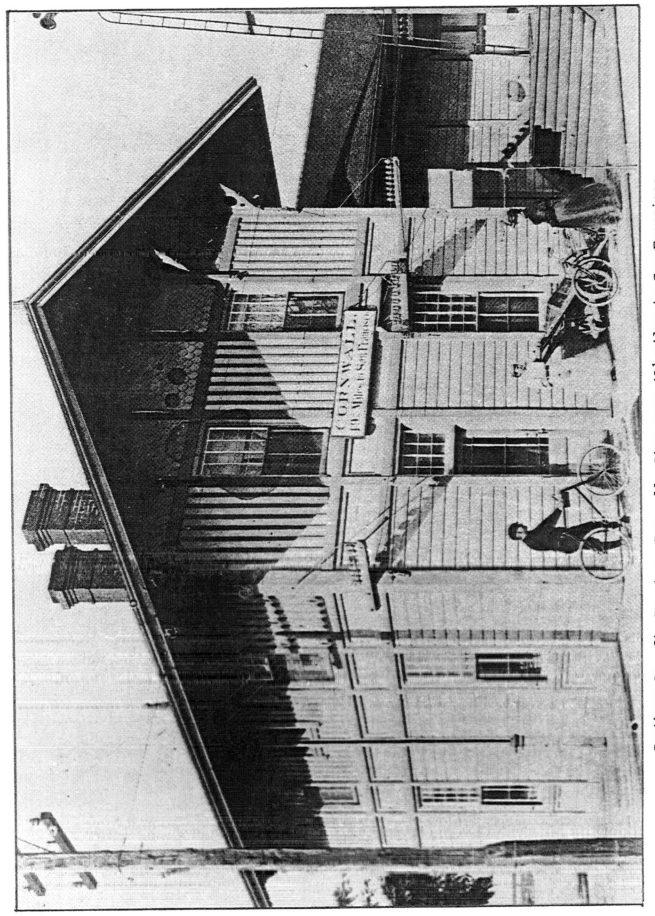

Southern Pacific Depot at Cornwall. Sign says 49½ miles to San Fransisco.
from Author's Collection

VALENTI ANGELO, MASTER BOOKMAKER, ARTIST AND AUTHOR

Valentine Angelo was born June 23, 1897 in Massarosa, Tuscany, Italy, a small village on the slopes of the Apennines, also known as the Little Alps. According to Angelo's autobiography many strange things happened at his birth. He said the church bell that had hung in the church tower for six centuries fell and almost put the village priest out of business. A fire in the mayor's house destroyed evidence that would have put the mayor on the gallows. He also said he attempted to sing the Italian national anthem. A man with a sense of humor.

When Angelo was very young, his father left the village to seek his fortune in South America and left his wife, Valentine and his younger brother to stay with his parents. It was at this time seven year old Valentine's life was influenced to follow his artistic future. As he remembered the incident, it happened at the school in the monastery where the village children were taught their lessons. One day as he approached the school, the old monk who was his teacher was sitting on a bench in the sun reading from an old book. As the monk would turn a page, his face seemed to light up and Valentine saw tiny flashes of light. When he reached the monk, he saw that he was reading from a fifteenth century manuscript, Book of Hours, entirely written and illustrated by hand. Each page was embellished with pictures in vivid colors and burnished gold. As the pages were turned, the sun on the gold made the flashes of light that Valentine saw. It was the most beautiful book in the world as far as he was concerned and he carried that conviction with him the rest of his life. He never was able to find another like it. The monk realizing young Valentine was interested in books and art, spent a lot of time showing him different kinds of books in the monastery library. The village wood-carver and painter, who saw his early attempts at drawing, encouraged

the young boy to spend time at his shop and learn more about art.

In 1905, the family made the move to the United States, staying briefly in New York City. They moved to Antioch in the Spring of 1905. The Angelo home was on the northeast corner of L and 6th Streets in the Prosserville part of Antioch. It was in the old wooden schoolhouse on G Street that the nine year old boy got a very small education. He had to leave school after three years to go to work on farms to help the family's financial situation. Val said in his autobiography that the young town toughs made his life and his younger brothers lives miserable with their cruel jokes. One of his brothers, Silva, was so affected by this that in later years became a prize-fighter just to settle accounts with the toughs. There were five brothers and two sisters in the Angelo family.

The Fibreboard paper mill was close to his home and this was where Valentine found an education. The paper mill's yard was filled with mountains of old rags, magazines and newspapers. The young boy hungered for learning and he made the most of the comics, Police Gazettes, periodicals and the various illustrated catalogs that he found in the yard. His next encounter with books came in 1906 when the Great San Fransisco Earthquake happened. One day shortly after the earthquake, boxcars full of books arrived at the paper mill yard. The mill personnel unloaded thousands of water-stained, charred and torn books but there were many in perfect condition. All had been through the earthquake and fire. These books were to be beaten into pulp and made into paper. Valentine spent many hours searching through the books and the mill watchman often helped him to find good books. In those books, Val discovered Shakespeare, Thackery and other great authors and pictures, words, dreams and visions. These books brought joy to him and helped shape his destiny. Angelo said they were like food to him and he read, read and re-read them.

Valentine worked at the paper mill until he moved to San Fransisco about the time of World War I. He worked at temporary jobs as a chef and pastry baker in the various hotels while spending all his spare time at the libraries and art museums. He studied at the San Fransisco Art School, situated where the Mark Hopkins Hotel is now located. During World War I, he was befriended by Charles Barrett, a famous photographer and lover of the arts, Barrett helped him get a studio in his building where Angelo set up his drawing board and easel and proceeded to establish himself as an artist.

In November 1920, his work was shown in Antioch. Twenty of his paintings and drawings were exhibited at the L. Meyer building at 2nd and H Streets. The Daily Ledger had this to say about the artist..."Angelo is rich in the heritage of a name that for centuries has been regarded as synonymous with the highest achievement in art. But apart from that purely accidental asset, he is endowed with greater gifts, a pure native sense of color, a feeling for the beautiful, and an energetic and perseverance nature that has won him a place as one of the most promising young artists in San Fransisco."

At this time some of his paintings were on exhibit in that city, notably, the painting, "Spanish Church", which was hung in the Palace of Fine Arts. Valentine also realized he was not going to make a decent living by painting at that time so he made up a portfolio of various illustrations and showed them to many art directors. He was finally hired by a photo-engraving firm and became a commercial artist.

While working for this company, Angelo continued his art studies at the California School of Fine Arts. There he met Maxine Grimm, an art student and they were married July 23, 1923 and their marriage lasted almost 40 years until her death in 1970. Because of her interest in the arts it was a long and happy union.

By a stoke of good fortune, his friend, Charles Barrett, introduced him in 1926 to Edwin and Robert Grabhorn. The Grabhorn Brothers Press had the reputation of printing only the finest of books in limited editions. Some of the greatest examples of printing came from their presses. By this time Valentine had dropped "ne" from his first name and was known as Valenti Angelo. He accepted their job offer although the money was 1/5th the salary he was receiving from the last company. The first book Valenti illustrated for the brothers was "The Letter of Amerigo Vespucci". It won the country's highest award for book design...the gold medal of the American Institute of Graphic Arts. He had found his vocation and from then on it was one book after another and one award after another.

The Daily Ledger had this story.... Painting By Local Artist On Exhibition....Two of the fifty outstanding books of the year from the stand-point of printing and typography were illustrated by Valenti Angelo, former Antioch resident. Of the fifty, six were printed by San Fransisco firms and it was two of this number illustrated by Mr. Angelo who also made the drawing for Walt Whitman's "Leaves of Grass" recently republished as a deluxe edition. Mr. Angelo's painting, "The Evil House", is now on exhibition at the modernistic show of the City of Paris, San Fransisco. It is highly suggestive of the John Marsh home at Marsh Creek and has attracted much attention among critics.

He worked with the brothers for six years and during that time he decorated, illustrated and illuminated forty five books and other documents.

When the Great Depression arrived there was no sales for the fine and rare book market and Angelo decided to move to New York City. He had made a connection with an art gallery while in San Fransisco and this association with the gallery decided his move. He started to paint again and his paintings sold well and this gallery handled the sales of his paintings.

His book illustration reputation had preceded his move to the big city and the Limited Edition Club soon hired him and he was kept busy for the next 34 years. His first work for the Club was Burton's "Arabian Nights Tales" which he did 1001 illustrations in each of 1500 copies of the book.

Next came "The Songs Which Is Solomons" that required hand painting in 23 carat gold the illuminations in 20,000 copies of the book. It took Valenti and his entire family months to complete the job.

In 1935, Angelo started his own book printing business using hand presses. Printing by hand is expensive with much waste of material but he felt that only the finest of books could be made by this method and his creations proved him right. During all this time he was busy with sculptures and paintings. Photographer Ansel Adams called Angelo's work "truly timeless". Author Sherwood Anderson once said..."his paintings are reaching for some lost dignity in man...and in reaching help bring it back." Sherwood bought two of his paintings and commissioned Angelo to do a portrait of his wife.

Valenti was also an author of children's books. In 1937 he illustrated a book for an editor of children's books at Viking Press and she asked him to tell her about his early life. His reminiscing intrigued her and she asked him to write every thing down. Three months later, Angelo handed her a 400 page manuscript titled, "Nino". After considerable editing, the book was published and it was the first of 17 children's books that he wrote and illustrated.

Angelo's wife died in 1970 and in 1975 he moved back to San Fransisco. Because as he put it..."I began to hear footsteps in New York, my wife's footsteps walking around in my memory.

I realized there wasn't much left for me there and I had to return to the place where I started." Valenti lived on Knob Hill in a small apartment where he continued to paint and print the rare and fine books that was his specialty. His sister, Rose, said she was amazed at how he managed to get the big press into one of the small rooms where he worked. The apartment was filled with almost 300 books-....many of them hand illumined in 23 carat gold, most of them printed on fine parchment in extremely limited editions. These are the kind of books only found in private collections and rare book libraries. All of these books bore the signature of Valenti Angelo...artist, author, illustrator and printer.

Valenti died in 1982 at the age of 85. He is remembered as a sweet, kind and loving man by his sister, Rose Kaylor of Antioch. A friend, Peter Hanft, Assistant Director of the Bancroft Library in Berkley, said Angelo always had a twinkle in his eye. All of Valenti's books are in the University of California's Library.

His two children carried on the Angelo artistic talent and tradition. His son, Peter, was a celebrated musician and his daughter, Valdine is an author of children's books.

Angelo at his drawing table, 1960.
Courtesy of his daughter, Valdine

53

These examples of Valenti Angelo's work and the photograph of him and his press models are courtesy of his sister, Rose Angelo Kaylor

BEFORE AN OLD PAINTING OF THE CRUCIFIXION · Carmel Mission, June, 1960

By N. Scott Momaday

Valenti Angelo   1975   San Francisco

Another small sample of Angelo's mastery of the printed work and his illustration of books

The Twenty Third Psalm of David printed by hand operated press and illustrated by Angelo. Gold leaf on words, THE LORD.

Valenti Angelo with few of his model presses

Angelo at work, 1963. Courtesy
of his daughter, Valdine

Valenti checking a peice of his
work, 1949. Courtesy of Valdine

LEDGER

VALLEY INFORMED ☆ ☆

SELECTED
FEATURES

, CALIFORNIA, MONDAY, NOVEMBER 28, 1932

WILL CUSSED IMITTEE

House Judicia-
Calls Meeting
er 2 to Frame

—

, Nov. 28. (U.P.)—
er of the House
ittee today an-
response to re-
emocratic leader-
led a meeting of
r Friday, Decem-
a prohibition re-

resolution to be
personally handed
aker John Garner.
proposed consti-
ent as made pub-
nan, provides for
accordance with
platform pledges.
ratification of the
pecial state con-
ld be for a period
rs.

PAINTINGS BY VALENTE ANGELO ATTRACTING ART LOVERS AND CRITICS TO BAY CITY EXHIBIT

Paintings by Valenti Angelo, former Antioch boy, have brought favorable comment from the well known novelist, Sherwood Anderson.

Anderson was so taken with several of the paintings of the local illustrator that he purchased one which now reposes in a place of honor over his desk in his study.

The writer declared that it was an inspiration to look at the picture by the Californian, and he made the following comment concerning it:

"It represents very perfectly what good paintings mean to me. Valente Angelo has been touched and moved by men at work."

Mr. Angelo now has an exhibit of his paintings and drawings at Vickery, Atkins & Torrey, 500 Sutter street, San Francisco, which has attracted many lovers of art. The exhibit has been favorably commented on by several well known critics and anyone from Antioch who visits San Francisco in the next week or two will find a great deal to interest them, because the creator of the work is a former Antioch resident.

The work is divided between painting and drawing, about a dozen examples of each. Most of the drawings are in red chalk.

A San Francisco newspaper comments: "This man knows what mining is. He has done it himself. Those fellows with stark simplicity of mein shows nearness to Mother Earth. They are symbols, too, and the little lamp they have on the cap suggests the Host in the Mass.

"Whether he depicts a brewery or a mine, the mean home of a toiler or ramping horses underneath the moon, you have the feeling of an artist of vision."

TU AS ARI

Antio
to
Pla
ma

Mrs.
charge
Associ
nounce
sent o
to citi

This
them
the cu
the
rate
are ca
by mi
advert
metho
becau
as ev
help t

A c
been
earne
at on
the

Senior Ball to Be Held Frid

56

IS MY FACE RED?

ADEMACHER IS

FRUIT AND VEGETABLE PACKING HOUSES

Antioch, Oakley, Pittsburg, Brentwood shipped vegetables, fruits and grapes all over the United States and the world, creating jobs for the local communities. The women, in particular, were able to make some money to spend on some of the necessary things dear to the heart without breaking the family budget.

Therefore, the packing and shipping warehouses and the canneries played a big part in the lives of the local families.

Wheat was first shipped from the docks of Antioch but it was the railroad that started the big move that made Antioch a major exporter of vegetables, fruits, nuts, grapes and some meats. The Santa Fe Railroad built warehouses at the foot of "G" Street in 1906 which were used by many companies to ship produce on their trains. (the first warehouse was built by Henry Beede who sold it to the railroad).

The Santa Fe Railroad owned the riverboat "Frances" that traveled up and down the Sacramento and San Joaquin Rivers to collect produce and brought it back to the warehouses for the various shippers. Among them was the Pacific Fruit Company, Earl Fruit Company, Tarantie Produce Company, Harry D. Roper (a quiet Englishman who was well liked by the Antioch community) and many more packers who used the Santa Fe warehouses to ship produce all over the world.

This was the earlier days before the canneries were established in Antioch.

Not only was the "Frances" used the bring the produce to the warehouses but sailing scows, schooners, steamers and barges were employed to bring the harvest to Antioch.

When the produce arrived it packed in ice and then loaded on the railroad cars to be shipped to eastern U.S. and European markets.

The Ledger always had headlines when the major produce was ready to be processed at the warehouses. One of these was "Grass", not to be confus

ed with today's marijuana, but it is asparagus. This vegetable was in great demand at the markets and it brought a very good price. In the 1920's the first asparagus of the season sold for $1.20 a pound.

This perennial garden vegetable of the lily family is a native to the Mediterranean area and is now grown all over the world. The tender shoots of asparagus are cut and shipped in the Spring.

Captain George K. Kimball first planted the vegetable on Kimbell Island across from Antioch. Later on, other families started to grow asparagus and it in time became one of the prime crops of the area. The rich tule land is ideal for the growing of asparagus as is the sand lands. The vegetable was a very profitable crop and still is although a great amount is now imported from Mexico due to the inexpensive farm labor available there.

Many of the canneries moved to Mexico to take advantage of the cheap labor.

Asparagus takes two to three years to reach maturity and it is then ready for harvest. The plant will produce tender shoots for approximately fifteen years. Harvesting in the Spring started at sunrise and it was and is hard work. When the shoots reached the height of nine inches, the workers bend over to steady the spear with one hand then cut it with a sharp knife using the other hand. The shoots or spears were then bundled and picked up. The spears grow quickly in the warm spring weather, as much as three inches a day.

When the tops are cut off, the spears regenerate extremely fast and many times the workers went back to the same field the next day and harvest them again.

In the early years, the farmer's children were out in the fields cutting asparagus for four or five hours before going to school. If the children got to the schoolhouse before 10:00 AM they were not marked as being tardy. When the children were in their teens

57

they worked in the packing sheds and canneries and they were allowed to be out of school for a half day. However, all missing school work had to be made up before the end of the term.

Besides the Santa Fe packing houses there were many other packers located in the Oakley, Pittsburg, Antioch and Brentwood area. None of these exist today and not much is known about their locations. One mentioned was the Meek Packing House that was robbed one night by five men who helped themselves to some asparagus and departed.

The Ledger said..."It was no wonder Eastern people pay fancy prices for this delicacy when robbers will risk their lives in order to obtain a small quantity."

Antioch Ice And Fuel, owned by the Donlon brothers, built a cooling building near the city wharf as it was found that by cooling the asparagus it would stay fresh over night. When the spears were cut in the morning, bundled and then picked up for transport to the packing house, it was to late to prepare the asparagus for shipping. The cooling building was the answer to keeping the asparagus fresh overnight. The Donlons also furnished the ice for packing the produce for shipping.

The men of Antioch and Pittsburg were employed in the fields. The Ledger said in 1906..."A number of men are going to river points to work in the asparagus and each day they may be seen departing. This class of help is doing contract work. Monday one crew of fifteen departed, all from the western part of town (Prosser--ville)".

Ninety percent of the world's supply of asparagus was shipped from Antioch and for years Antioch was known as the" Asparagus Capitol of the World".

Another business that prospered in Antioch's early years was the manufacture of wooden boxes to pack the produce for shipment to the eastern market.

The Signal Supply Company had their box factory in Antioch and the plant was considered the most modern of it's kind in the West. The company manufactured some of the best quality of boxes used in the state. Being located at the gateway of the Delta, it was particularly situated to handling the box business of the islands and it was also advantageous to growers of all kinds of products requiring crates.

Many of Antioch's men and boys were employed in the various box factories.

About this time in the 1920's, lettuce came into the picture as a major crop. The first shipments of lettuce were produced at Bouldin Island and shipped from Antioch to the Eastern markets. Fifty acres were first planted to find out how many carloads it would produce. The fifty acres filled forty railroad cars.

The Bloomfield barges hauled the crop to Antioch and the Santa Fe warehouses. There it was prepared for shipment and the produce was packed a little different from other products. The outside leaves were stripped from the heads of lettuce and the heads were then placed in crates that were half filled with ice.

Antioch and Stockton were in competition for the permanent shipping point for the Delta lettuce. It was decided in Antioch's favor when the Antioch Fuel and Ice Company made an offer the shippers couldn't refuse.

Celery was another crop that was shipped from Antioch in great quantity It was grown in the islands and because of our climate it matured during the Christmas season and was in great demand for the holiday dinners.

Most of it was grown on Jersey, Twichell and Sherman Islands. Also there were large fields in the Stone, Holland and Hotchkiss Tracts. Antioch had the reputation of producing the highest grade of celery in the region.

The majority of the celery, starting in the first weeks of November, was transported on the Bloomfield Brothers' barges. Celery shipped from here was 75 percent of the United States supply.

Potatoes, onions, beans and other crops were harvested and shipped in abundance from Antioch. Fruit and grapes were a big business. Pears, mostly Barletts, came to Antioch to be packed and shipped to the Eastern markets in July. The Ledger in July 23, 1921 said the Steamer "Frances" had brought down from the upriver districts enough pears to fill one hundred railroad cars. Some shipments included plums.

The Pacific Fruit Exchange and the Earl Fruit Company were the heaviest shippers. Apricots always brought a good price for the growers and the "cots" reached Antioch in the late spring.

Around August, the Tarantie Company packed table grapes at the Santa Fe warehouses for shipment to the East. The first grapes ever sent from California came from the Antioch-Oakley area except for the Thompson seedless which was grown in San Jose.

The local area grapes were the Flame Tokays and in 1922 the growers were getting $75 a ton for them. That was a good price as the crop ran 6 tons to the acre.

Among the local growers was Douglas, Mettier, Dragon, Ruiz and Minaker.

The packing houses were the main Antioch business for shipping produce until the first of the canneries arrived.

In 1921, the first cannery was built in Antioch. This was the R. Hickmott Canning Company.

The first Santa Fe packing warehouses built 1906. Steamer, "Frances", docked at warehouse. Charles Bokakel Jr. Photo

New Santa Fe packing warehouses. Piling is from old warehouses. (Note the Antioch Hotel back of warehouse. Fred Stamm moved it to that location from 2nd Street when he built the El Campari- Theater in 1928.) Photograph 1940 From Author's Collection

60

EARLY CANNERIES AND THEIR EMPLOYEES

Canning is the preservation of food involving the placing of food in containers providing an airtight seal and then sterilizing the containers and their contents with high heat. Heat is necessary to destroy bacteria, mold and yeasts and the airtight seal prevents contamination and spoilage. How effective this method of preservation was proven by scientists. William Parry, the English explorer on his third Arctic Expedition in 1824, left cans of roast veal, vegetables and gravy in the Arctic In 1911, cans of meat and pea soup that had been left by Parry 87 years before were opened and found to be fresh and eatable. In 1938, English scientists opened more cans, now 114 years old, and found them all in excellent condition.

In 1795, France was at war with England, Prussia, Austria, Spain and Sardinia. France was winning the war but losing soldiers and sailors lives due to scurvy and malnutrition. France offered a prize of 12,00 francs to any person who could devise a new and successful way of preserving food for a long period of time. After 14 years of experimentation, a French chef, Nicholas Appert, won the prize in 1810. He successfully preserved fifty kinds of foods by sealing them in airtight glass jars and heating them in scalding water. He also stressed cleanliness as part of the process.

The next improvement was the use of iron and tin canisters for the preservation of food. The hand-blown wide mouth jars with their wired and waxed stoppers were difficult to handle and seal. The English who recognized a promising outlet for their iron foundries, developed the iron and tin canisters. Peter Durand patented his metal container calling it a canister from the Greek word, "KANASTRON", meaning basket of reeds. In the early nineteenth century, reed baskets were used by the English for storing tea, coffee, spices, fruits and vegetables. Durand found this word a natural for his container and gave the currently accepted name of canning to the process of sealing foods and sterilizing them by heat. The Yankee bookkeepers and salesmen shortened canister to "can" and the word came into recognized use.

Before the turn of the century, cans in the United States were made by hand from heavy tin plated iron using hand held shears. The body was rolled and then the side seam soldered and then the bottom and top were joined and soldered to the body. A hole was left in the top in which the food was filled in the can. When the can was filled, a tin disk was soldered to the top and it was now ready to be processed. This type of container, known as the "hole-in-top" can could be made at the rate of 60 cans in a 10 hour day. This was displaced with the "sanitary" can made with crimped and locked seams. By 1874, An American by the name of A. K. Shriver invented a closed steam pressure kettle that allowed controlled high temperatures and cut the time of processing to a new minimum.

Mechanical improvements were being continually made in the harvesting and canning of the raw product. By 1921, the developing of methods for soaking, washing, sorting, and grading, in the blanching, in peeling and coring, in filling and exhausting, in sealing and processing, and cooling hot cans made the processes almost automatic. Moreover, the new development of conveying systems between the machines also aided in the speed of processing.

There were many fish canneries in the area but the decline of the fish in the Sacramento and San Joaquin Rivers lead to their closure in the early 1900s. Information is more complete for the two canneries in Antioch that operated until the late 1970s. These two canneries specialized in fruits and vegetables.

R. Hickmott Canning Company was the first cannery built in Antioch. The date was 1921. Robert Hickmott was called the "father of asparagus canning". He experimented in canning asparagus in the early days by cooking the "grass" in a wash boiler on a furnace made of bricks under a willow tree. From this modest beginning worked up a business that became a power and shipped the Hickmott brand products to all parts of the world.

Hickmott had a total of four canneries before the one in Antioch was built. The first one, built in 1882, was on Bouldin Island, No.2 and No.3 were also on Bouldin Island No.4 was built in Orwood Tract.

When Hickmott's No.4 cannery burned down in the Orwood Tract, the corporation that owned it decided to build a new No.5 in Antioch. Work on the new cannery started in the first part of 1921 and it was planned to be finished in time for the start of the asparagus season in April.

Work proceeded rapidly and the old machinery formerly used at the old No.4 cannery that survived the fire was brought to Antioch and installed with many pieces of new equipment, all being of the latest and most approved design. With arrival of a pile-driver, work was started on a new wharf, which was used for receiving and transferring asparagus and other products from river boats to the main building. The products were carried along the wharf on an endless ball-bearing electric conveyer, almost an eighth of a mile long, that went under the Sante Fe Railroad tracks straight to the spray room in the main building where the washing process took place.

The main building was constructed of reinforced concrete and was 117 by 217 feet. The greater part of the work was carried on in this structure and everything was arranged to insure speed and connivance. From the spraying room, the asparagus was trucked to the sorting tables, where the workers sorted and discarded all imperfect stalks. This was important as not a single bruised or discolored stalk was used. From the sorters, the product passed to the canners, who placed it in cans. These cans were placed on a conveyer, which carried them through what is known as exhaust boxes at the rate of 42 cans a minute. This equipment does the sterilizing and places hot water in the cans, giving them the vacuum previous to sealing, which is done automatically.

The first sealing machine clinches the cover, the second rounds the edge and the third operation rolls the seam so tightly the can is made air-tight. The cans were placed in the cooker, where they remained for 22 minutes, after which they were placed in the cooling room. After remaining there for 5 or 6 weeks all cans were examined for leaks, after which they were labeled and boxed previous to being stored in the warehouse.

The warehouse was also built of reinforced concrete and was adjoined to the cannery on the west side. It could handle 65,000 cases and the old brick distillery buildings were also used to store the canned products. They were able to store 15,000 cases in them. The distillery buildings were opposite the cannery building and a spur track of the Sante Fe passed between them. A number of freight cars could be loaded at the same time from the cannery and warehouse concrete loading platforms.

The cannery was equipped at that time with 4 exhaust boxes, 4 sealers, and 5 cookers. Heat for the cookers and hot water was furnished by 2 tubular boilers located in a powerhouse, 45 by 40 feet. Water for the cannery was supplied by 2 large storage tanks, one holding 150,000 gallons. From this tank the water passed to a settling tank of 30,000 gallons, and from there it went through a chlorination process, then filtered through 2 rapid sand filters. From there it was pumped to various parts of the cannery. The plant had many fire hydrants and dozens of fire extinguishers as part of their fire protection plan. The new cannery cost $175,000.00 to build.

The R. Hickmott Canning Company was a corporation composed of both Americans and Chinese business men, 60 % of the stock was owned by the Americans and the remainder by the Chinese.

When the cannery opened for the season's asparagus pack in 1921, even though the buildings weren't quite finished, there was a labor problem. The workers were all Chinese, there were 140 of them, which caused quite a protest to be made by the local people. Insults were hurled and some cannery equipment was destroyed one night. The Antioch Ledger of April 9, 1921 had an editorial chastising the local 'people for their actions. The editor pointed out that the corporation at the very start told the town that they had a 5 year contract to use Chinese help and it had one more year to run. After the contract was finished they would hire local people to work the cannery. In 1922, Hickmott started their packing year with mostly Antioch help.

Also in 1922, the cannery stated to process fruit and installed a "peeler" to pare the skins from the fruit.

In 1925, Ferd Stamm built Hickmott a new concrete warehouse, 70 by 170 feet, south of the spur track that served the cannery. That year the asparagus pack totaled 100,000 cases and 270 persons were working that season. Hickmott Cannery was in continuous operation for 58 years under various owners.

Penrose Russell was one of those owners. "Penny" Russell first worked as a plant superintendent for Vince Davi at Western California Cannery. Plans failed for Davi and Russell to purchase another cannery as partners. Russell then bought the Hickmott Cannery in 1955 from the Parrott Company. Russell's son, Renny, worked at various jobs for his father and finally became the general manager. After sale of the cannery to another corporation who failed , it reverted to the Russell Trust with Renny in charge. It was finally closed in 1979.

Over the years it has canned asparagus, shad roe, pork & beans (packed especially for the Armed Forces during World War II), Apricot and apricot nectar, peaches, fish (processed in a separate building called the "fish house") and tomatoes. Much of Hickmotts canned foods were sold under contract to Safeway Stores.

At one time the property was worth about 6 million dollars.

In 1934, the Ledger had a story of the daily pack of asparagus for the Hickmott Cannery. James Dunn, superintendent, announced it would be 3500 cases per day. His assistant was G. W. Dempsey. They planned to operate two daily shifts of 250 persons totaling 500 employees per day starting in early April.

Wednesday, Feb. 7, 1934 Daily Ledger had this story.... "V. A. DAVI TO OPEN CANNERY IN WAREHOUSE. BRANCH OF WALNUT CREEK CONCERN PLANS TO START OPERATIONS BY CANNING ASPARAGUS......

Painting and cleaning the interior of the old Signal Supply Company's warehouse on L Street and the Sante Fe tracks started yesterday, so it can be occupied by the Western California Canners Inc., of which Vincent A. Davi is president.

Mr. Davi formerly was employed by the Booth Company in their Pittsburg cannery, and several years ago he established his own business in Walnut Creek.

Because of Antioch's location and since the warehouse was available for use as a cannery, Mr. Davi last week leased the warehouse from the Sante Fe Company, the present owners.

The building is approximately 80 feet wide and 300 feet long. Antioch city water will be used in operating the new enterprise. Pipe has all ready been purchased and is at the wharf ready for installation as soon as ditches are dug on L Street from Second to the plant. It will take 400 feet of pipe to complete the line. Work will begin on it next week.

There are two spur tracks to the warehouse, which is well built and ideal for the installation of modern canning machinery.

Asparagus, fruit, tomatoes and possible preserves will be canned at the plant. It will give employment to around 125 people, and will be operated in addition to the Walnut Creek plant. It is understood that canning such a variety of products, it will be kept running most of the year.

Associated with Mr. Davi are Bert J. Davi, secretary-treasurer; Estelle Enea and R. E. Cotter, directors."

On March 9, 1934 there was more news of the cannery. A crew of seven machinists and carpenters started working on the old Signal Box Company warehouse (they built shipping crates for the early packing warehouses) on February 19. Bert Davi was in charge. Machinery was moved from the Walnut Creek plant and additional equipment was purchased. Evidently, the original news article about the Walnut Creek plant being in operation at the same time as the Antioch plant was in error.

One reason the firm decided upon Antioch as a location was the excellent water available here and, also, railroad and water transportation helped in their decision. The availability of additional fruits and vegetable in this area for canning was a big factor too.

The Western California Canners opened ahead of their schedule of April 1. The canner code laws decreed the operations to start on April first but the asparagus was developing so fast there was a surplus so all canneries were given permission to start the season earlier. Western started operations March 24, 1934.

Their first pack was 300 cases and that increased as the season progressed. The first crew was 150 persons.

The asparagus canning season of 1934 employed approximately 800 East County persons at Hickmott and Western California canneries.

In 1935, Western California constructed a warehouse on the south side of the plant. It was 125 by 75 feet and the contractor was G. Seeno of Pittsburg. It was made so the refrigerated railroad cars could be run into the plant and be loaded from either side. The cannery doubled it's capacity with installation of $25,000 of new machinery

The cannery employees came from Pittsburg, Antioch, Oakley, Brentwood and other parts of East County to work in the canneries of Antioch. Most of the workers were women (about 80 % or more) and the additional income was most welcome. Also, the seasonal work gave them more time to be with their children. During the off season time , they could collect unemployment benefits. Husbands didn't complain because it wasn't a regular job in their eyes and the money was needed income for the family. For many years cannery jobs were probably the best work the women of East County could find in the 1920s, 1930s and early 1940s.

The minimum age for the workers in this era was legally 16 but although the cannery owners did not knowingly hire anyone under age, some times the girls prevaricated about their age to work in the cannery. Children looked forward to the possibility of cannery work. They admired the ladies and the uniforms which were neat, prim and which all the workers wore.

Employment in the canneries was hard work. The jobs were deafening, exacting, rigidly supervised and was accomplished while standing on the concrete floors. Cuts on the hands and arms from the sharp knives was an occupational hazard. The days were 7 to 8 and sometimes 10 to 12 hours long and were five to seven days a week according to the supply of produce..

Many of the workers started working at a young age (12 to 13 years old) in the produce fields and packing sheds and lived through the Great Depression. This experience produced workers that knew the value of working as a way of life. They seldom called in sick and were always on the job.

While the work was hard there was a comradeship among the cannery workers that was hard to find in any other work place in East County. They had a close knit family environment which included parties, potlucks and sing--a-longs. It , also, was a chance to meet friends and future boyfriends. Both canneries encouraged a family feeling among their respective employees.

There was no racial problems at this period in time. The workers were of Italian, Spanish, Portuguese, Mexican, Puerto Rican, Chinese, Filipino, "Okies" and some black women. They had fun and sang songs together

while working. The singing was in Italian, Spanish and English. During lunch times, the ladies sat outside eating their lunch, trading recipes and doing a little gossiping.

The women were proud of their labor and were competitive because many got paid for piece work and got a bonus for producing more than required. The esprit-de-corps among the women of Hickmott and Western California Canneries probably was never surpassed anywhere in the world.

Bruna Checci O'Berry remembers going to Hichmott Cannery with her father, who owned a bakery, when she was a little girl in the late 1920s. During coffee breaks, the women came out to his Ford bakery truck to buy his hot rolls and donuts. Bruna said she was allowed to go into the cannery and she was given as much fruit as she could carry.

"Male" jobs at the cannery such as electricians, warehouse men and machinery workers weren't open to women until the 1960s because of contracts the canneries had with the Teamster's Union.

Laura San Martin, an Antioch resident, worked at Hickmott Cannery from 1940 until it closed in the late 1970s. She did work at other jobs during World War II but was an employee of the cannery for most of those years. She has fond memories of Gordon "Mac" Mc Cuish, who was the cannery's superintendent from the 1930s until 1948. Laura said when they had parties "Mac" would join in with the crowd. When the canning season started "Mac" would call all the employees together and give them a nice pep talk. He treated all the workers like they were part of a family and that made them work even harder for "Mac". San Martin said that in later years, around the 1950s, it got to be mostly production work due to the increased mechanization of the cannery. However , she said, even at her age today, she would still like to work at Hickmott if the cannery was in business.

Gloria Martin was a young girl

(13 years old) in the 1950s and she recalls the many times she had to clean her mother's white shoes. Every night when her mother came home from the cannery, young Gloria's chore was to make the shoes white again. She said it was quite a problem to remove the tomato seeds that were wedged in the seams of the shoes and remove the stains left by the fruit. She used a toothbrush to work the seeds out of the seams. Then she had to use the white shoe polish to renew the shoes. Her mother was Lupe Romo who originally worked in the packing sheds packing asparagus. Lupe worked at Hickmott and also for a short time at California Western. She returned to Hickmott and ended her 17 years in the canneries there. While at Hickmott, Lupe became an Avon distributor and all her customers were the cannery ladies. She would take their orders at the cannery and deliver the products to them at the cannery. Gloria said this extra money bought a lot of nice things for the family.

Lavina Gori Russo's mother first worked at the asparagus packing shed and she brought little Lavina to the job with her. She was placed on lug boxes beside her mother when there was no baby setter available. In those early days this practice was allowed. Mrs. Clorinda Gori went to work at the Hickmott Cannery when it opened for business in 1921. However, when Western California Cannery started operations in 1934, it was to her advantage to take a job there. Clorinda Gori's home was on 6th Street just a few blocks from the cannery site and she walked to work. Bill Ostertag, the plant superintendent and a relative , finally got her to retire at age 70. Lavina said her mother was the only one who wore the cannery cap in the proper manner.

James Davi started to work at California Western in 1935 while still at college taking a business course. He was at home during the mid-term time and was looking for a temporary job. He had been working at a fish canning company in Pittsburg but that job stopped when the fishermen went on strike. He had two months left on his mid-term leave so he went to Antioch to apply for a job at California Western. Jim was dressed in his good suit when he went to Antioch. He was hired on the spot and was told by Bert Davi (a cousin) he had to start work immediately so he took off his coat, rolled up his sleeves and started to work.

After Jim worked for about three weeks Vince Davi asked him for more background. What type of studies he took at college , accounting etc. and how long before he graduated. Jim said he had a year before graduating. Vince then said they had a problem because they needed someone to take the place of an office worker who had suddenly quit. His new duties included just about all the office work necessary for the cannery's operation. His wages were $57.50 every two weeks.

Two weeks before Jim was due back to college he gave notice of quiting. Vince said they need him to work until Christmas and would he consider working until then and suggested Jim talk it over with his father. Jim's father felt Jim had received more experience and knowledge working at the cannery than he could get if he went back to college. Also, the cannery was paying for this experience and knowledge. Jim Davi continued working for Vince Davi.

That Christmas when the bonus checks were given to the salaried employees, Jim received a surprise bonus of $250 plus a substantial wage increase. He received many salary increases during his long years with the company and never asked for any of them. In quick time, he became the office manager at a very young age . Jim worked for California Western Canners for approximately twelve years.

Hickmott Cannery in 1921 after completion.

River boat being loaded with vegetables for Hickmott Cannery

One of Western California Canners retort ovens

Group of Western California Canners workers.

Hickmott Cannery workers photographed in 1927.

Boilers of Hickmott Cannery.
Courtesy of Renny Russell

Workers at sorting table. Courtesy
of Margaret Del Pozo

Buffalo-Vac used for making tomato paste.
Courtesy of Renny Russell

Cannery workers at the can loading ring.
Courtesy of Margaret Del Pozo

Cans filled with tomatoes coming off the loading ring.
Courtesy of Margaret Del Pozo

Hickmott Cannery after being closed in 1979.
Courtesy of Renny Russell

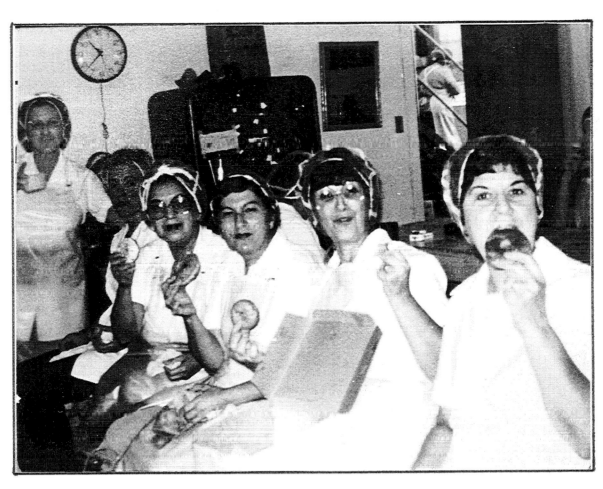

Cannery workers on their lunch break.
Courtesy of Margaret Del Pozo

Western California Canners. Buildings in background with smoke stacks.
From Author's Collection

72

THE BEGINNING OF THE LAW AND OFFICERS

The pioneers arrived in Antioch before the law. Dr. John Marsh, the area's first white American settler, had numerous disputes with outlaws on his Los Meganos Rancho (near what is the town of Brentwood) in the 1840s. He got into trouble when he contracted with a vigilante group to eliminate some trouble makers. As towns sprang up in Contra Costa County, the town trustees drew up codes and ordinances to cope with lawlessness ...from this the peace officer came into existence.

Peace officers included sheriffs, constables, marshals and police officers. The sheriff's office, the chief law enforcement of the County, was charged in general with the keeping of peace and the execution of court orders. The constable was the peace officer in a township, town or village with powers and jurisdiction somewhat less than a sheriff. The marshal. a minor officer of the law in some towns, usually collected taxes and polls. The police was the governmental department of a city organized for keeping order, enforcing the law and preventing, detecting and prosecuting crimes.

Contrary to popular legend, Marshal Wyatt Earp was only a deputy marshal and had no jurisdiction outside of the small frontier towns where he was employed. His reputation was fabricated by the writer, Ned Buntline.

Our early law officers were men of courage and willingness to use a gun. A peace officer knew he might have to act immediately and usually had the right to do it.

At times, the sheriff or deputy sheriff was called into the towns and villages to enforce the law when the local officer was unable to do the job. Many times the constables and marshals were deputized by the county sheriff with authority to make arrests outside of their jurisdiction. A six-gun and a tin badge was their uniform.

Contra Costa County's first peace officer was Nathaniel Jones who was elected for a two-year term as sheriff on Oct. 7, 1850. Antioch and the immediate area furnished five sheriffs.

The first sheriff from Antioch was Roswell B. Hard, who held the office from 1867 to 1869. On October 1868, an earthquake badly damaged the courthouse and jail in Martinez. The county supervisors immediately authorized Hard to build a jail in Antioch, but today no record of it being built exists. (Hard was also Antioch's first mayor in 1870).

In 1875, Fred Wilkening, an Antioch saloon keeper, became sheriff and served until 1877. From 1877 to 1879, David P. Mahan was elected sheriff. He was the operator of Antioch's Brentwood Brick Works. He was also the town marshal in 1873. From 1885 to 1889, James Rankin of Sommersville held the sheriff's office. He owned the Union Hotel and general store in Sommersville, a general store in Nortonville and later bought the Sommersville Mine.

After Rankin left office, R. R. Veale, a farmer near Antioch and a deputy sheriff, became sheriff...the office he held for the next 40 years. During his tenure, Veale captured many an outlaw at gun-point but never killed a man. He was so fast with a gun that no one could "out-draw" him. He was known as a real gun slinger, with courage and determination, and he always got his man, arresting him and letting the law take it's course.

Contra Costa County Jail in 1877 was a terrible place. The editor of the Ledger had this to say about the jail..."POORLY VENTILATED...Last Monday while in Martinez, we accepted an invitation from Sheriff Wilkening to visit the County Jail. At present there are only four persons confined within it's walls and grates, yet with even this unusually small number, it was plainly evident that there is great lack of proper ventilation. The damp dark cells are loathsome with a fetid air, to breathe which quickly poisons the blood and is destructive of health. Every human being , it matters not how great a criminal, is by divine right entitled to air and sunlight and neither the individual nor a community has a right to deprive a fellow being of either. If the felon is deserving of death, behead, hang or shoot him ; but do not destroy him by a slow process of poisoning by withholding the free air and light which alike it is the privilege of man and beast to enjoy. It is simply inhuman and barbarous to compel any person to breathe the poisonous, filthy atmosphere of our County Jail".

Antioch was incorporated as a town on Feb. 6, 1872. This was when records were started and reliable information was available about law and order. On March 14, 1872, the town trustees drew up the first four ordinances. Antioch's first ordinance was one prohibiting owners of livestock to let them run at large within the town's limits. Ordinance No.2 was to fix and collect a poll tax of $1 from each male inhabitant within the limits of town. Ordinance No.3 determined what was nuisances and gave the authority to prevent and punish same. Ordinance No.4 protected dwellings from destruction by fire from defective flues.

Some of the other early ordinances passed included one that banned looking at an opium smoker for fear of a fine "not over $100". Another was not to disturb the peace by driving or riding horses through the streets at an immoderate or unusual gait of speed. One limited the first railroad to enter the town to a five mile an hour speed. Children (under age of 16) had to be of the streets by 9:00 PM.

There isn't much information about law in Antioch before the town was incorporated, but the town was known to have had a jail. One of the first trustees' meetings instructed Sheriff Hard to repair and furbish the town prison, which was not to secure. The Ledger reported on one incident..."Escaped....The Chinaman who was incarcerated in the town jail this week for misdemeanor, through the chicanery of some sympathizing brother, broke through the planking and sloped."

George A. Swain was Antioch's first peace officer in March 1872. He was sworn in as the first marshal of the newly incorporated town and he became one of Antioch's most effective officers. He resigned in June 1872 and became a constable of the sixth township that included Black Diamond (Pittsburg), Antioch and the surrounding area. The first day policeman was James Cushing. On May 2, 1872, Thomas Sutton was hired as the night watchman. Some of the townspeople complained that Sutton didn't do his job. He was eventually replaced by William Long. Sutton was rehired in June, 1875 but fired the next day because he was not a U. S. citizen. Fred Wilkening was hired to replace him.

On April 3, 1872, the trustee board meeting received bids for the feeding of prisoners in the Antioch jail. The bid of E. Nelson of 24 cents a meal per prisoner was accepted. Marshal C. McMasters was authorized at the same meeting to notify people living within the incorporated limits of the town of Antioch having defective flues, stove pipes or chimneys to conform to Ordinance No.4 and No.5 forthwith.

Antioch's marshal's pay was 25 dollars a month plus 8 percent of all taxes and license fees he could collect for the town. His job was an elected one, the other peace officers were appointed. When making an arrest of an individual with a reward for his apprehension, the officer was allowed the keep the money. In 1870, the newspaper reported that Sheriff Warren Brown arrested a murderer named Wells who had a private reward of $5,000. The story was ended by saying..."a profitably day's work for Sheriff Brown."

Constable Swain was one Antioch's more notable peace officers. His activities were covered quite comprehensively by the Ledger. For example, in 1872, just the fear of Swain arriving quelled a Chinese riot in Antioch's Chinatown. He closed a house of prostitution in Nortonville and took the women to San Fransisco.

Another story by the newspaper headlined..."A Disgraceful Cutting Affair" displayed his courage. "It occurred at the Bank Exchange Saloon between parties who had been engaged in the alluring game of poker. Four or five persons were in the game and the claim to the "pot" lay between Frank Beard and Uriah Mayfield, familiarly known as "Kentuck". The latter went in with two aces and drew another one, while the former held three kings and drew nothing. He then called "Kentuck" who showed his three aces and proceeded to take the money which lay on the table. This Beard protested against, averring that there was foul play and he wasn't going to be robbed, at the same time securing the coin and putting it in his pocket. Of course, hot words was the direct resultant, great passion ruled. A fight started and Constable Swain started to break it up when Beard drew a big knife, which struck Swain in the face inflicting a three-inch cut just missing his right eye. This knocked Swain to the floor and Beard managed to slash "Kentuck" a number of times before Swain could get back in the fight. Beard was disarmed and the wounds of the two men were sewn up and dressed by a doctor. Beard was charged with two counts of assault with a deadly weapon."

Swain was sent after many a desperado and usually got his man or woman. He was known to track down, capture and arrest two or more criminals at a time. Many of the incidents involving officers were not big crimes but rather minor alterations such as assault and battery. For example, in one case reported in the Ledger, a Mrs. Goulding was arrested for assaulting and battering Robert McClanahan. The story read..."She was brought before Judge Mayon, who after mature deliberation, concluded that the charge accorded with facts, and he sentenced

her to pay a fine of $15. Another charge against her...threatening etc...-..was dropped on condition that she "wouldn't do it again". It costs money here to pound a man's jaw with a rock."

Other early peace officers were E. B. Whelihan, James Thomas, John D. Turner, Mr. Long, Nat Cleaves, Tom Shine, Charles A. Sweeney and D. M. Pitts.

At the turn of the century, Antioch lawmen began to find their workload ever increasing and thus new methods of enforcement were developed. Some of their problems were a result of the newly invented automobiles. Lawmen now had to deal with automobile accidents and enforcing the rules of the road, such as speed limits.

World War I brought gambling and prostitution to the fore. Although Antioch and Pittsburg had more than their share of these vices before the war, they accelerated. The problem was noted in the January 1918 town trustees' meeting minutes. The Standard Oil spokesman said the soldiers guarding the Standard Oil Tank Farm (at the southeast corner of Sommersville and Buchanan Roads in Antioch) were rendered inefficient by intoxicants and gambling.

Constable E. B. Whelihan tried repeatedly to get the town trustees to pass ordinances prohibiting gambling, saloons and houses of prostitution, but was told to enforce the laws already in effect. Whelihan did just that with a vengeance. Meanwhile, the trustees renewed and granted more liquor licenses...almost at every meeting from 1872 until 1921.

On March 24, 1913, the trustees ordered the marshal to keep regular office hours at city hall from the fifth to the tenth day of the month to collect taxes and water bills.

Tom Shine was the town marshal from 1908 until January 7, 1914, when he died eating supper at his home. Although the Daily Ledger chastised Shine for not performing his duties the way the newspaper perceived he should, he held that position for six years.

When Shine died, Charles A. Sweeney was sworn in as marshal on January 9, 1914. His starting salary as marshal was $89.99 a month. His office was a side room in his home at 206 W. 6th Street. The house is still there. Sweeney was a former marshal, whose first term began in 1885. A big man with a bushy mustache, he was well--qualified. Sweeney made a raid on Antioch's Chinatown in 1885. He raided an opium den owned by Ah Sing on Front Street (now Riverview Walkway) and arrested five Chinese man. He was also appointed deputy sheriff for Antioch and vicinity in that year. Sweeney served a term as town clerk starting in May 1899.

Evan T. Thomas, whose nickname was "Yant", was hired as night watchman in 1916. "Yant" was a character and, one time, He got into an argument with "Fat" Friemering. Yant was quite inebriated and pulled his gun. Fat ran for cover, taking shelter behind the wooden base of the flag pole in the center of G and 2nd Streets. Yant began firing at the base and when Fat counted six shots, he ran and hid in the tules by the river. Yant's father-in-law, W. Bloomfield, ordered him to hand over his gun and he did. This incident didn't cause him to lose his job.

On July 20, 1915, the town trustees had Sweeney swear in four deputy marshals, who had absolute authority at fires. they were M. S. Rodgers, F. Linwood, Ed Edenberg and W. W. Belshaw, all who were Antioch volunteer firemen. They received no pay for being special deputies.

"Yant" Thomas resigned in December 1918 and Nat Cleaves was hired to replaced him. Cleaves got a pay raise, the old salary was $60, to $100 a month.

On February 28, 1921, Ordinances No.50A and No.51A were passed. Ordinance 50A prohibited gambling in the saloons and 51A prohibited the sale of liquor. Prohibition had arrived and Antioch was observing the law.

However on May 16, 50A was repealed. All the saloons and bars applied for soda licenses to replace their liquor licenses. They were going the stay open and, according to the older residents, the saloon keepers and bar owners sold bootleg booze. Marshal Sweeney was ordered to enforce the ordinance prohibiting the sale of liquor. He was authorized to appoint four deputy marshals to help enforce the ordinances and they were to serve without pay.

The new automobile and the laws governing it's use created the traffic officer. Antioch's first speeding arrest occurred in March 1913. The Daily Ledger said it was a good idea to arrest speeders because the law was disregarded daily, not only by strangers, but by the townspeople.

Automobile registration in 1914 cost from $5 to $20 for 60 horsepower and above. Speed limit was 30 miles per hour on the country roads, 20 miles in thickly populated territory and 15 miles in town. Vehicles were required to have two white lights visible 500 feet in front, One red light visible 500 feet in the rear, and a white license plate light, all which had to be turned on one hour after sundown and turned off one hour before sunrise. Muffler cut-outs were not permitted in town. All fines were paid to the treasurer of the city or county and the money eventually placed in a road fund.

The Contra Costa County traffic patrol was organized in 1918. This was the first highway patrol and five or more Antioch residents were in the patrol. They were John Cox, Dick Trembath, Thomas "Red" Dungan, Bud Doyle and Earl Hoyt. In 1922, uniforms were added and, in 1925, the State Legislature created the present California Highway Patrol and placed all county patrols in that department. Captain George "Little Giant" Becon was the commander of the county patrol and later was made captain of the CHP in Martinez. In 1929, The Highway Patrol boasted 280 uniformed officers,

76

80 white painted Model A Ford coupes and 225 four-cylinder Indian motorcycles. Seldom were there more than 100 patrolmen on duty within the state or more than two or three officers on duty in Contra Costa County at the same time.

Charles C. Golden, who was originally a night policeman, became Antioch's first traffic officer sometime in 1927. He had to buy his own motorcycle, an Indian bike equipped with a speedometer, light and a siren. When he resigned in January 1930, the city bought his motorcycle for $299 and paid him an additional $51 for the speedo, light and siren. When Officer Golden resigned, nine Antioch men applied for the job, and Tom Dungan got it. He later became a California Highway Patrol officer.

An indication that Antioch was about to have it's own police department came in a mention in the trustees' minutes of the August 8, 1927 meeting that a police commission had been formed. On August 18, 1927, the Daily Ledger reported that the State Legislature passed a law at it's last session that made the board of trustees a city council without making the remaining trustees councilmen. With the passage of the law, the chairman of the board officially became the mayor of the city and City Marshal Sweeney became Chief of Police. So as of August 1927, Antioch had one chief and one night policeman, Charles Golden.

The Ledger editorials spoke out against bootlegging, gambling and prostitution. The editor urged the city council to instruct the police officers as to which law violations should be cause for arrest. The newspaper editorial said..."Unless instructed to make arrests for gambling he (the police officer) can watch and participate in gambling games and never say "boo". Unless instructed to arrest bootleggers and drinkers he can drink with the violators. Unless instructed to arrest reckless and speeding drivers he can calmly watch

them endanger the lives of others." The editor said..."a new understanding was needed" so that the officers would make arrests for every violation, not taking it upon themselves as to judge whether the individual is a good fellow, whether his home is here or if he is a stranger. The officer must enforce the law and not otherwise."

Shortly after the editorials ran, Officer Golden arrested five men for disturbing the peace and for the possession and sale of liquor.

Although Antioch had a police department in 1927, Constable "Yant" Thomas was still on duty as indicated in a newspaper story that year. The story reported on Thomas's trip to Susanville in Lassen County to bring back two thieves who had stolen Liberty Farrace's auto in Antioch.

On May 3, 1928, the police began enforcing parking laws. The yellow one-hour parking signs had been installed for several months but the laws were not enforced until then. Another full time officer was hired. Officer Golden began working the day shift and bought himself a motorcycle to enforce the traffic laws. M. G. Stephens of Stockton, an experienced officer, was hired to be the new night officer. Stephens would later become Antioch's second police chief. Stephens and Golden made the first appearance of the police department in uniform. Meanwhile. the services of a part-time officer by the name of Buck were discontinued.

Within the first two weeks of the operation of the enlarged police department, 24 arrests were made...all for traffic violations except for one man who was looking for a place to sleep. To keep the records straight, he was charged with an offense before allowed a berth at the City Hall Jail. Traffic fines also made a dramatic increase. The first month the city judge took $107 in fines, and fines later increased to an average of $500 a month.

The police department experimented

with a new lighted stop sign which was erected at 4th and L Streets. It was placed above the regular stop sign.

According to newspaper accounts and many old-timers Officer Golden was a mean and tough man which led to his downfall. He was not above a little scam. For example, when an automobile accident occurred, and a tow truck was needed, he always called for City Councilman Christiasen's tow truck. If the competition's tow truck arrived before Christiasen's did, Golden would run him off.

Golden was called before the city council several times to explain his actions. His involvement in a shooting at one of the bawdy houses resulted in his resignation. Called to break up a disturbance after a man said he was robbed at the Dahnken Hotel, Golden fought with the victim (Clyde Nichols) and then pulled his gun and shot him in the thigh. After the District Attorney advised Golden he was planning to take the matter to the Grand Jury for investigation, Golden resigned. As a result of this disturbance, the Redlight Abatement Law was enforced and four hotels allowing prostitution were closed including the Dahnken Hotel.

The city council passed a resolution to install a red light and bell, operated from the telephone office, to call the night officer when needed. The bell and light was placed on a tall pole at 2nd and G Streets.

In 1930, Thomas "Red" Dungan was hired to replace Golden, but only a year later he resigned to join the California Highway Patrol. The Ledger article said...."He got a new fancy uniform and brand new Harley-Davidson motorcycle with a broad springy seat and a speed of 90 miles per hour." Dungan was quoted as saying..."He felt like a French general on dress parade."

During his tenure, Chief Sweeney and his son, Charles Sweeny Jr., captured a notorious bank robber, Frank Brazil Jr. The chief showed a picture of the robber to his son who recognized him as a man working at the paper-mill when the son was working the traffic detail there. The duo took Brazil into custody and notified the San Fransisco Police Department, which had a warrant out for his arrest.

Charles A. Sweeney handed in his resignation on April 29, 1930 after serving in law enforcement for 50 years. He continued, however, to serve as city marshal and tax collector. On Thursday, May 1, 1930, M. G. Stephens became Antioch's Chief of Police and the two patrolmen, Harry A. Woolcott and Al LeRoy , along with police clerk, Belva McElheney, were appointed Deputy Chiefs of Police. Their monthly salaries were $175 for the chief, $150 for the deputy chiefs (patrolmen) and $75 for the deputy chief (clerk).

Stephens was chief until 1934. Next, LeRoy was made Antioch's chief of police and held that position for 10 years before Harry Boyer was appointed chief in 1944. Boyer was chief for 15 years and was replaced by E. A. "Hap" Carlson in 1958. Carlson remained chief for 21 years and raised the department personnel of 25 men and 17 police reserves to the highest degree of efficiency. He retired in 1979 and was replaced by Len Herendeen.

FRANK BELL
Announces himself as a candidate for the office of
TOWN MARSHAL
Election: April 13 1908

M. G. AZEVEDO
Announces himself as a candidate for the office of
TOWN MARSHAL
Election: April 13, 1908.

T. P. SHINE
(present incumbent)
Announces himself as a candidate for the office of
TOWN MARSHAL
Election: April 13, 1908.

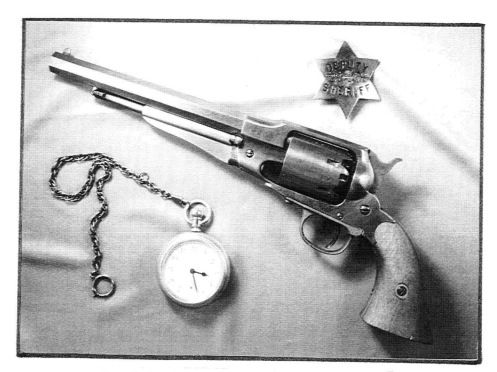

Total Equipment for early lawmen, a gun
and badge. From Author's Collection

Lawman C. A. Sweeney in white duster, Constable E. D. Whelihan,
third from the left. 1915   From Charles Bohakal Jr. Collection.

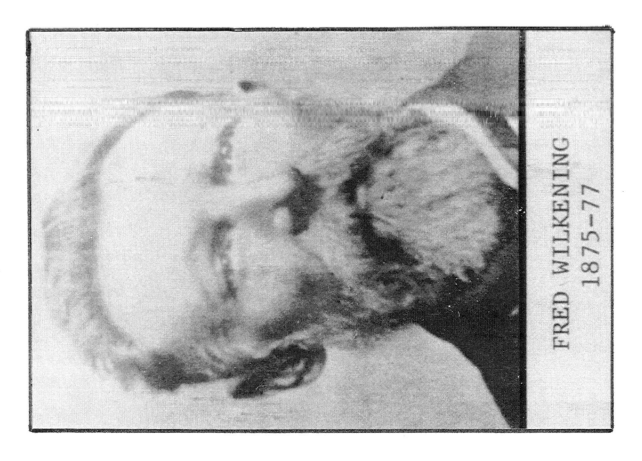

FRED WILKENING
1875-77

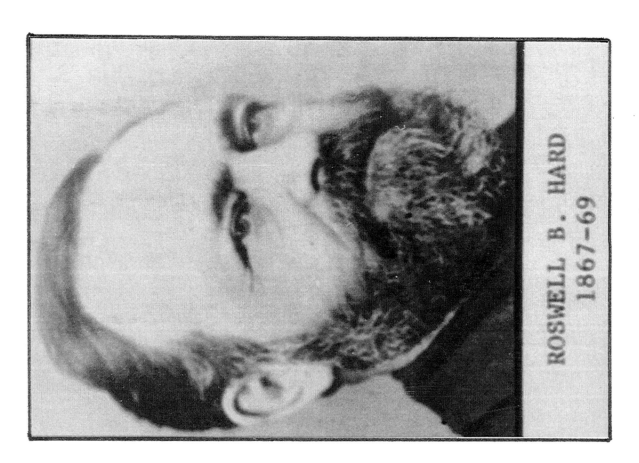

ROSWELL B. HARD
1867-69

Sheriff's photographs are from Contra Costa County Sheriff's Collection

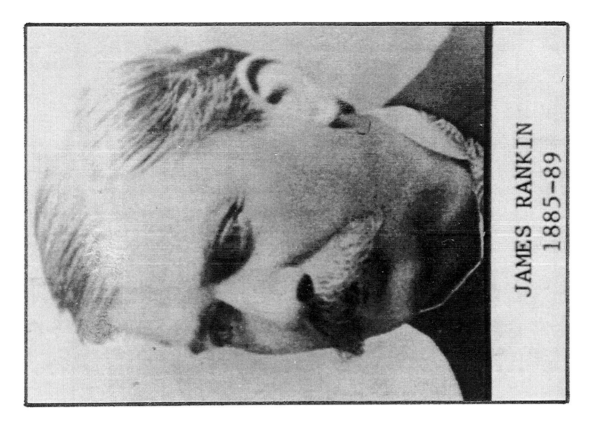

JAMES RANKIN
1885-89

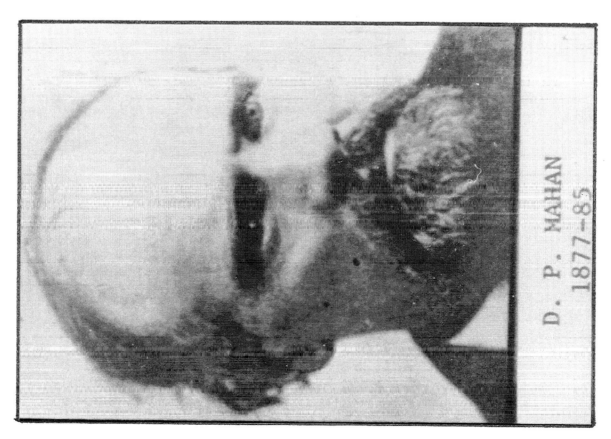

D. P. MAHAN
1877-85

She=iff's photographs are from Contra Costa County Sheriff's Collection

C. A. Sweeney, Marshal, Deputy Sheriff and Antioch's first Police Chief. A lawman for 50 years. From Author's Collection.

R. R. VEALE
1895-1934

R. R. Veale, Contra Costa County Sheriff for 40 years. From C.C.C. Sheriff's Collection.

Contra Costa County Traffic Patrol
badge became California Highway
Patrol badge in 1929. (Note Stephen's
and LeRoy's cap badge.)
From Authors Collection.

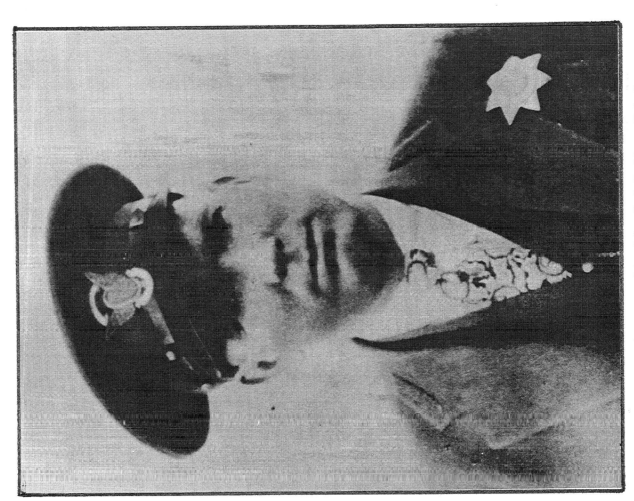

M. G. Stephens, Antioch's 2nd Police Chief
1930-1934. From Antioch Police Department.

Al LeRoy, Antioch's 3rd Police Chief, 1934-1944
From Antioch Police Department Collection

Jake Ackerman, one of Antioch's
first motorcycle officers. 1925
From Author's Collection

Johnny Cox of Antioch, 1937, officer of California
Highway Patrol. From Author's Collection.

85

California State Highway Patrol, Contra Costa County Patrol, 1933 photograph.
Capt. George "little Giant" Beacon, left front row. From Author's Collection

ROSWELL BUTLER HARD, MAYOR AND SHERIFF

Roswell Butler Hard was one of Antioch's leading citizens in the early days of the town. However, he is somewhat of a mystery since little can be found about him, though his red brick home still stands and is one of Antioch's most historic landmarks.

Hard was born at Jericho, Vermount, on Aug. 29, 1829. He married Leonora Humphrey and they moved to California in 1852, locating in or near Oakland, where he raised livestock and worked as a butcher. Soon after arriving he joined the Oakland Eden Lodge of the Free and Accepted Masons.

Some 12 years later, in 1864, Hard withdrew from the Eden Lodge. On June 15, 1865, he became a charter member of the Masons' Antioch Lodge No. 175, probably about the same time he became a resident of Antioch.

When the Antioch Lodge held it's charter installation, Nov. 4, 1865, Hard was installed as the first Junior Warden and served as Worshipful Master the next year and was a dedicated Freemason. Though a butcher by trade and county sheriff, in 1869 he had built the big two story house and several commercial buildings.

Hard was influential in county politics and served as Contra Costa County Supervisor 1866-1868. He was elected Sheriff of Contra Costa on Sept. 5, 1867, winning over his opposition, William C. Srail, by 94 votes out of 1322 cast. According to county records, he continued to serve as a Supervisor during this time.

On Oct. 21, 1868, the Martinez Courthouse and Jail was severely damaged by an earthquake. The top and rear walls of the building collapsed and extensive repairs had to be made. The County Board of Supervisors authorized Sheriff Hard on Oct. 23, 1868, to build a calaboose (jail) in Antioch and set aside funds for it's construction. However, there no record of it ever being built. Evidently, the old jail was repaired swiftly as the Grand Jury of 1869 commended Hard after finding the prisoners were

in good condition and well-fed.

The office of sheriff paid good money for those days. Two entries in the county's expenses showed Hard was paid $991.00 on Nov. 13, 1869 and on Feb. 12, 1870 he received $484.-80. He was elected for a second term as sheriff from 1869-1870.

While sheriff, Hard started to build on his Antioch properties. He owned six lots in the town, lots 9, 15, 18, 19 , 20 and two-thirds of lot 14 all in Section B6. His large two story brick house was built on lots 14 and 15 at 815 First Street

Bricks for the house came from Antioch's first brick factory located nearby. According to a story in the Contra Costa Gazette of May 22, 1869, the house was almost ready for occupancy on that date. The story reported..."Among the recent improvements in Antioch is the large and handsome, two-story brick dwelling house of Sheriff Hard, which is now approaching completion. With the exception, perhaps, of the Marsh House, and that recently erected by the Fish brothers at Martinez, Mr. Hard has the handsomest and most costly house that has yet been built in the county, and it is gratifying to see, among those of our citizens who can afford to do so, a disposition to expend money liberally in providing handsome and comfortable homes."

Hard built another two story brick building in Oct. 1869 as reported in the Contra Costa Gazette of that year. The newspaper reported..."The occasional visitor at Antioch cannot fail to notice the progress of improvement, and the indications of business activity, which distinguishes that place from most all others in the county. Since a previous visit earlier in the season, we noticed when there a few days since, the addition of a number of nice frame dwellings and several frame stores; the completion of Beede's brick store, a spacious and substantial structure, and the near completion of a fine two-story brick building for Sheriff Hard.

This building has a frontage of 40 feet and is 50 feet in depth; affording two stores on the ground floor, 12½ feet in the clear and a fine brick and cement cellar below. The upper story, which is to be prepared for offices, will be 11 feet in the clear; and the building altogether will add much to the substantial business convenience of the place (Antioch)."

Then again on April 9, 1870, the Gazette reported..."We met with a cordial reception from our brothers of the Ledger and spent a pleasant half hour with them in the new print office. In the evening we interviewed the Social Club, and assisted citizen Galloway, in defeating citizens Hard and Southwick, at a rubber of Whist...- The Social Club has a fine large room in Hard's new building, well lighted and warm, furnished with a small library and periodicals; and is a pleasant and orderly social resort for gentlemen by whose fixed monthly contributions it is supported." (This building in all probability became the Tyler Hotel on I Street, then named Main Street.)

By 1871 Antioch was about to become incorporated. A petition was circulated and signed by 102 voters. Among those who signed were many men who were destined to become leading citizens of Antioch. Among them was Stamm, Hard, Abbott, Wilkening, Wills, Levy, Mahan, McCartney, Galloway, Donlon, Swain, Homberg, McMasters and many others. Of this group, Hard, Wilkening and Mahan were county sheriffs at one time. On Feb. 6, 1872, Antioch became incorporated, and as such, the town could now pass laws, collect taxes, have police protection, etc.

The governing body was known as the board of trustees and the presiding officer was the president. (Today they are called the city council and mayor.). The first board of trustees met March 2 in the living room of the Hard residence and elected Hard as Antioch's first mayor. Mark S. Levy was appointed clerk to record their minutes... a wise choice because

his penmanship was beautiful and the minutes are very easy to read even today.

The very first ordinance passed provided that..." It shall be unlawful for any person to drive or lead any horse, mule, jack, jennie, ox, cow, calf or any other animal upon any sidewalk in town." Most of the sidewalks were made of wood and unable to support the heavy weight of these animals.

At this time Hard was considered a businessman and rancher. He was very active in the affairs of the area and was vice president of the Contra Costa Farmer's Club in 1870.

Antioch's Assessment List of 1872--1873 showed Hard as having $1,500 in goods, two horses, one cow, one pig, one $75 watch, $120 in cash and three buildings.

Hard also owned a sheep ranch near Deer Valley, according to a news article in the Contra Costa Gazette in 1869. In addition he was a partner in R. B. Hard and Co. that owned stock in the Antioch Petroleum Co. He and his partner, Sam Brown, dissolved the company Jan. 31, 1868. His county return in 1867 showed he made $2,673 for that year.

The last known mention of Hard is in the 1878 records of the Antioch Masons when he withdrew from the Lodge. According to some accounts, Hard died in Alaska in December 1885 while on a gold mining expedition with a group of men from Martinez. The Alasken Record of Vital Facts has no record of his death nor does Contra Costa or Alameda County Register of Deeds.

ROSWELL BUTLER HARD

Contra Costa County Supervisor, Sheriff and Antioch Mayor.
Courtesy Charles Bohakel Jr.

Sheriff R. B. Hard's home at 815 First Street, Antioch. Mrs. Hard standing by the porch. House is still standing today at this location awaiting restoration by the City of Antioch.

Courtesy Contra Costa County History Center

ROGER'S POINT (SMITH'S POINT)

The "Point" was named by William Wiggins Smith in 1849 when he and his twin brother, Joseph, purchased two half-sections of land and started the town of Antioch, which was first called Smith's Landing. The first mention of Smith's "Point" was in 1850 when the Pulsifer brothers, Deacon John and Dr. Joseph, laid claim to some land east of Antioch, (still known as Smith's Landing) and started a large vegetable farm on the flats above the "Point". They built a simple wooden pump to draw water with the aid of a windmill on the "Point" and produced large amounts of vegetables on their farm that they shipped to Sacramento, Stockton and San Fransisco.

Frank E. Peabody owned the "Point" in the 1800s. Robert Harkinson purchased the property from Mr. Peabody on July 5, 1902. He built a two story clapboard house (later, it was clad in shingles) on the "Point" facing the San Joaquin River. It had a lower porch and a glassed-in upper porch facing the water. The ground was excavated to situate the house so it faced the river. The house was entered from the upper story which had a dining room with no windows and three bedrooms. The lower part of the house contained the kitchen and sleeping quarters of the Chinese cook. Mr. Harkinson's study or retreat was also on this part of the house with a fine view of the river. From 1902 until 1939, the "Point" was known as Harkinson's Point. Frank was a prominent Antioch citizen and the secretary-- treasurer of the Bank of Antioch which was established in 1891.

He used the "Point" as a recreation getaway. It's location in an uninhabited part of Antioch made the stress of business life seem faraway. The "Point" was a great place to spend a vacation with fishing in the river, swimming in the little cove with the sandy beach or just watching the river traffic of scows, sailing vessels and steam boats. When Mr. Harkinson died, his sister inherited the "Point" and at her death it was passed on to her daughter, Maude B. Roberts.

After renting the property for quite a period of time, on September 21, 1939, John "Jack" Rodgers and his wife, Virginia bought the "Point" from Miss Roberts for a small sum of money. Mr. Rodgers was a prominent Antioch citizen and the owner of a large insurance agency. They remodeled the old deserted house into a Spanish type hacienda. It was a showplace and the Rodgers held many parties there for the social and political leaders. The grounds were like a park and many peacocks roamed the property. Rodgers' daughter, Virginia Calisesi, as a child found arrowheads, wampum and other Indian relics on the grounds.

In researching the boundaries of the property deeds, the California State Lands Commission wanted a name for the Point and Rodgers used his name. Now the Point was named Rodger's Point and it so remains today.

After "Jack" Rodgers death the property was sold and went through several owners before being purchased by the City of Antioch with plans to make it a public park.

The magnificent painting of the "Point" was discovered years ago back of several lockers or file cabinets in the old City Building by city employees. It had been "lost" for many years. The painting was by a very famous artist, Warren E. Rollins, who did the work in 1881.

Rollins was a resident of Antioch when he painted the "Point". A letter by artist to the editor of the Antioch Ledger in the 1950s confirmed that this untitled painting was of the "Point". He implored the city to buy that painting from the lady who owned it. It is believed that she donated the painting to the city at some time in the past. Also in Rollin's letter he mentioned painting a portrait of a reprobate sailor living on the "Point" by the name of Mitchell. This must have been Captain Mitchell, a mariner, living east of Antioch, who donated his ship's galley for Antioch's first school house.

The painting of the "Point" was in bad condition when discovered, having three tears in the canvas and it was covered with dirt and soot. The city donated it to the Antioch Historical Society in 1976. A grant from the Dean and Margaret Lesher Foundation in 1994 made the restoration of the painting possible and it was then discovered that it was a priceless piece of art and that Rollins was an internationally famous artist. (I discovered the letter authenticating Rollin's "Point" while doing research on another historical article.)

This magnificent gold framed glowing 4 by 5 foot piece of art is now on loan to an art gallery.

Virginia and John "Jack" Rodgers. 1960
Courtesy of Virginia Calisesi

The Harkinson house on the Point in 1920. Courtesy of Virginia Calisesi

The Rodger's home on the Point looking at it from the San Joaquin River side.
From the Author's Collection

World famous artist, Warren E. Rollins' 1881 painting of the Point before restoration.
Courtesy of Ledger-Dispatch Newspaper

A grant from the Dean and Margaret Lesher Foundation made restoration possible.
Courtesy of Ledger-Dispatch Newspaper

In the earliest of civilizations, the delivery or transportation of news was of prime importance to the rulers of states and countries. These persons jealously guarded the income from the profits from carrying the mail. The postal services became state monopolies.

The earliest written missiles were pictographs embossed on clay tablets that were then baked to harden them. Later, writing known as cuneiform was used and this was adopted between 2500 and 2000 BC. The increasing power of the city states created the need for runners to carry these messages. The distances were what the runners could accomplish per day and at the end of the distance was a station or post guarded by soldiers. Later, couriers on animals were the carriers. They rode horses, mules camels and dromedaries between posts and as the first rider approached, a second one would take the pouch and head off for the next station or post. The transportation of news and letters by this method became known as a postal service.

The United States Federal Post Office was established at San Fransisco in 1848. Kit Carson made the first overland mail delivery from coast to coast in that year. It was difficult to deliver mail to the western towns from the eastern United States. The Butterfield Stage Line carried mail from St. Louis to San Fransisco. Their first stage coaches were of the Concord type carrying four passengers, their luggage and 600 pounds of mail.

The sailing vessels and steamers carried mail from the East Coast to San Fransisco. The opening day of the San Fransisco Post Office happened to coincide with the news of the gold strikes. The crew of the first mail ship, "California" which arrived about that time, deserted the vessel to search for gold. After this, the mail ship crews were kept aboard by force. Service on the overland mail routes improved so much that it surpassed the erratic ocean vessels schedules.

The first adhesive backed stamps were issued in 1847. One was a 5 cent stamp depicting Benjamin Franklin and the other one was a 10 cent with a picture of George Washington. Advertised letters were those left uncalled for at post offices. The postmaster would have the letters' addressees listed in the local newspapers and they cost an extra one cent when they were claimed.

The fabled Western Pony Express ran from St. Joseph to San Fransisco and took $10\frac{1}{2}$ days to make the trip. When the rider reached Sacramento, he boarded a steamboat for San Fransisco. If fog delayed the boat along the way, the rider got off at the nearest wharf and rode his horse on to the Bay area and San Fransisco. The charge for the Pony Express Mail route was $5.00 per half ounce.

Railroads revolutionized the Postal System in 1864. Mail was picked up "on the fly" by the train from track-side mail cranes. The mail was then sorted in 40 foot especially constructed mail cars. Mail now usually arrived on time.

U. S. Mail in 1849 was delivered by boat to Antioch at the wharf at the foot of J Street. This wharf was built by William W. Smith so he may have been the acting postmaster for Antioch at that time. The first post office in the area was at New York of the Pacific, officially known then as the "Junction". This post office was moved to Antioch in 1852 and was located on 2nd Street between H and I Streets. Captain G. W. Kimball in 1052 was the first appointed Antioch postmaster. The above information was found in local history. On the other hand, the official United States Postal Service history doesn't show any postmasters listed before 1855. According to the Service, George R. Clarke was the first appointed postmaster in January 18, 1855. The next two were George Brown, November 2, 1855 and Job C. McCaster, October 5, 1857. Captain George Kimball was then appointed postmaster in 1861.

Mail was very slow in the early days as the editor of the Ledger proclaimed in one of his 1870 issues. He said he received a letter on Tuesday in a Wells, Fargo and Company envelope mailed on the previous Thursday from Martinez. He said a lame bull team would have brought it sooner.

Three early Antioch postmasters were Russell Eddy-1863, David W. Woodruff-1864, Van W. Phillips-1875. The location of these postmaster's offices are unknown.

A Mr. Black was the postmaster at Sommersville in 1885 and received his mail from Antioch. He had his office in his store which sold fancy goods, papers and periodicals. The store was located next to the Union Hotel in Sommersville.

From 1867 til 1875, Stephen Abbott and Jay Tuttle were Antioch's postmasters and their office was also in their drugstore. They spent a considerable amount of their own money converting part of their store into a post office. The government did not pay for any post office or equipment until later years. The Ledger said the men's office was the neatest and handiest one imaginable as any in the State. There was 3 windows, one 5 feet by 4 feet for receiving mail bags and express matter, one for the convenience of the telegraph operator and another for general delivery. There was 60 private lockboxes for mail. Although the Ledger had both men as the postmasters, Stephen Abbott was the appointed postmaster

In 1887, Josiah Rio Baker became postmaster and his store on the northeast corner of 2nd and G Streets was his office. He was a hard working, accommodating and gentleman postmaster. Baker held this appointment for five years.

David P. Mahan was postmaster from December 1885 until April 1889. Mahan was the Conta Costa County Sheriff in 1879.

Josiah Rio Baker was appointed postmaster again for another four years in April 11, 1889. David McCartney was next from 1893 to 1900.

The Post Office Department advertised for bids to carry mail from Antioch to Oakley and back. It was to be carried the distance of seven miles daily except Sunday. This advertisement was in March 1899. The Ledger said the people out in the sand country deserved a daily mail. Also in Nov. 1899, The Post Office Department notified Antioch telling them to commence weighing all mail matter passing through it's office. Mr. David McCartney was the postmaster then.

The railroad mail service was a big complaint about this time. There was only one mail train a day through Antioch to San Fransisco and that train passed the town at two o'clock in the morning.

Once again, Josiah Rio Baker on December 10, 1900 became Antioch's postmaster and held the position for 13 years. His time in the Postal Service totaled 22 years.

The mail service to Sommersville was discontinued in Feb. 1908 although mail was to be carried to Nortonville as usual. The Postal Service said the Sommersville residents could continue receiving mail if they put a mail box on the nearest rural route to their residences.

Parcel Post Service started at Antioch in January 1913. The Ledger story said..."like all other places, the Antioch Post Office began handling Parcels Post business on January 1st and although the local office was not swamped with packages a lot of them were sent from there. The Ledger had the honor of sending out the first package and E. B. Sellers of Oakley received the first package in the district. Seller's package weigh two pounds and cost only ten cents to mail." The cost within the Postal District of any post office was a local rate of five cents for the first pound and one cent for each additional pound. Out in the country, the parcels could be delivered by the rural carriers.

One of the interesting regulations concerned the rule about perishable articles that could be mailed. In that class was butter, lard, fresh meat, dressed fowls, vegetables, fruits and berries. Provisions were made for carrying almost every article produced on the farm except live animals and live fowls. Packages could be insured for up to 50 dollars. In 1916, the Fish and Game Commission banned the shipping of wild game by parcel post.

Alice M. Wall was acting postmaster from 1913 until 1914. Antioch had Postmaster James F. Saunders and assistants in 1914. The Ledger story in 1914 said they were the busiest people in town during the Christmas season, handling the hundreds of letters and packages and there was no doubt that this was the biggest volume of mail ever handled in the history of the town. Saunders was complimented on his handling of the mail even though he was inexperienced. Although he was considered a very obliging and competent postmaster who served the patrons willingly and courteously, he was indicted by the Federal Grand Jury of San Fransisco in 1916 on charges of embezzlement. Saunders was arrested and released on bond. His assistant, Miss Bessie Wrightman, was appointed acting postmaster on April 30, 1916 and she selected her brother, Ray, as her assistant. He had been the purser of the Lauritzen Transportation Company.

When Saunders was brought to trial many months later, he was found innocent of all charges. the newspaper story said he had lost his job and had paid the price of being indicted by the government. Miss Wrightman, in the meantime, had been appointed permanent postmaster of Antioch on June 27, 1916 and the post office was now located on 2nd Street next to the Antioch Meat Market. The building and equipment was owned by Gabe Meyers at that time.

The next big news was that of Antioch becoming a second class post of-fice. The town had to have a population of 3,000, sidewalks and houses numbered. The town already had more than 3,000 people and the sidewalks needed, the numbering was accomplished in short order. So, on July 1, 1919, Antioch became a second class office and the residents got free mail delivery to their homes. Letter boxes were erected around the town when the free delivery service was installed. Miss Wrightman was given three clerks, two who were carriers, to be paid by the government and her salary was also considerably increased. When Miss Wrightman resigned, Margaret Dorman was appointed acting postmaster for a month in 1920.

Up to 1927, the postmaster's position was decided on whether the Republicans, Democrats or some other political party was in power. The job was a political football until it came under the Civil Service Act.

The newly installed Aeroplane Service arrived in Antioch on July 1924. The first Aeroplane Mail received here was on July 1, 1924 and was a letter to Charles H. Mohr from his mother in Norwalk, Connecticut. It was mailed at 7:00 PM on July 1st. and arrived at Antioch during the night of July 3rd and the cost was 24 cents. After that date, Aeroplane Mail for Antioch people arrived daily. Envelopes had to be marked "Aeroplane Mail". Later the name for this service was changed to "Airmail".

The first mail planes were modified Curtis JN4s (called Jennies) and DeHavilland DH-4s and flown by Army pilots. These airplanes were World War I vintage aircraft. There were a great many crashes and loss of lives during the first few years of this service due to the type of airplanes used and the lack of navigational aids. The mail was flown in all kinds of weather which made for dangerous work. Later, the Postal Service used their personnel and airplanes to fly the mail. Finally, contracts were let to the airlines to carry the mail. The airfield used by the mail airplanes for departure from this part of the country was located in Concord. The mail was brought from San Fransisco in time for the 8:45 AM take-off of the airplane to Chicago. It was a 21 hour flight to Chicago and it took 30 hours to fly from Concord to New York.

In 1934, Postmaster General Farley canceled the airlines contracts due to air mail scandal charges brought against the airlines and the Army planes were again utilized to fly the mail.

The famous World War I ace , Eddie Rickenbacker, flew the last heavy load of mail from the Pacific coast in a civilian transport plane landing in Newark, N. J. on February 19, 1934. The wartime ace landed the huge twin motored air liner down on the field thirteen hours and four minutes after the take-off from Grand Central airport, Los Angeles, Calif. He had set a new world record for the flight.

The Army planes stripped of their machine guns and bombing racks and their holds bulging with mail were on the line ready to carry the United States mail on February 19, 1934. The flights were flown in all kinds of weather without pause. By March 9, 1934, eight of the fliers were killed in crashes in less than a month after the Army assumed the airmail service.

Col. Charles A. Lindberg told the committee investigating the air mail problems that the Army Air Corps pilots were sent aloft with the air mail without sufficient preparation or proper equipment. He said the Army pilots were given ten days to take over something that the commercial airlines operators had taken ten years to accomplish .

It was not long before the commercial airlines were back delivering the United States air mail

By 1928, Antioch was in need of a new and larger post office for which the Postal Department would sign a lease of 10 years. All equipment would be furnished by the Department. They received three bids including one from the Masonic Hall Association. Otto E. Klengel's bid was accepted. The building was built according to government blueprints by George H. Field on the G street site next to the telephone building located on the northwest corner of G and 4th Streets.

The move to the new post office was made on Nov. 1, 1928 by Postmaster Alice Webster and her staff. All equipment had be installed including 899 small and 44 large lock-boxes, all equipped with combination locks. The Ledger said the box holders were having a merry time trying to get their mail from the new boxes. They were seen singly and in groups working away at the combinations. One man of ranking intelligence got his open in $\frac{1}{2}$ hour of diligent effort. The paper concluded their "tongue-in-cheek" story by saying those who have their mail delivered by carrier pass by and smile at the box holders. After nine years as Postmaster Alice Webster resigned and Frank J. Biglow became postmaster in 1929.

The next new post office building was constructed by George Stamm at the corner of 4th and F Streets in the 1940's. William Westley Field was the postmaster at that time.

This is the early history of the Postal Service and the personnel who built Antioch's postal system into what it is today. My thanks to Postmaster Carolyn Hill who furnished the official United States Postal Service roster of the early postmasters which helped sorting out the dates of when postmasters were appointed.

100

Antioch Post Office in 1887 was in this building.
Postmaster J. Rio Baker on right in straw hat.

A STREET SCENE, ANTIOCH, CAL.

Early Antioch Post Office building on left. Sign
barely visible between the two trees.

Mail Carriers in 1911. Uniforms were not worn in those days.
Smithsonian Institution postcard

1913 Parcel Post Mail truck with two mail clerks and driver
Smithsonian Institution postcard

1902 DeGroot U.S. Mail truck. Engine was inside body.

Horse and buggy on rural U.S. Mail route. 1800's

1927 Rural Carrier delivering parcel post mail.

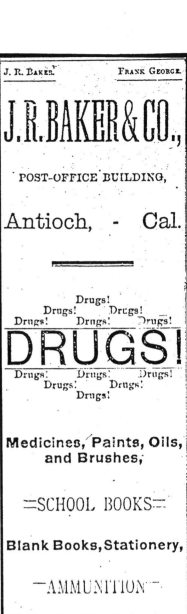

De Havilland DH-4 mail plane at Concord Airfield in the 1900's.
Courtesy Contra Costa History Center

ARRIVAL A N D DEPARTURE OF MAIL
Antioch Post Office

West Bound Arrivals

8:00 A. M.	3:00 P. M.
10:30 A. M.	7:00 P. M.

South Bound Arrivals

8:00 A. M.	1 P. M.
	6:00 P. M.

West Bound Departures

7:30 A. M.	8:30 P. M.
10:45 A. M.	4:80 P. M.
	6:00 P. M.

South Bound Departures

8:00 A. M.	1:00 P. M.
9:45 A. M.	5:00 P. M.

Railroad Mail Schedule

UNCLAIMED LETTERS

The following letters remain unclaimed at the Post Office at Pittsburg, Cal.:

Domestic—Hughes, Jack; -Harvey H.; Warren, Floyd C.; Martin, W. A.; Boyd, W. F.; Pinkerton, W. Jr.; Matheson, Geo., Jr.; Shields, H. I.; Gunlefinger, W. J.; McCarthy, John (3); Wilson, Pearl; Jones, E. H.; Brackbill, P. E.; Wood Mabel; Fanning, James M.; Thorne, J. E.; Mehat, A. Z. Dr.; Karlash, Ed.; Street, Mr.

Foreign—Frunento, Maria, Cardirelle, Guiseppe; Lucido, Antonina Prolo; Dimaggo, Gaetano Nona; Lucido, Fracesca Mera; Ramio, Gaetano; Russo, Stephano; Picetti, Arbamo; Lucido, Marcco; Bronzizi, L.

These letters will go to the Dead Letter Office, Washington, D. C., Feb. 8, 1917.

M. L. ROYCE, Postmaster.

Dispatch want ads get results.

Unclaimed letter notice

The first U.S. Airmail Service flight, May 15, 1918. Curtis-Wright JN-4 airplane This flight started continuous scheduled air mail. Courtesy Smithsonian Institution

LOADING CHEYENNE MAIL AT SALT LAKE

Loading Mail from Cheyenne, Wyoming on U.S. Army Air Corps airplane at Salt Lake City, Utah. Army carried Air Mail from Feb. 10 to June 1, 1934

Courtesy Smithsonian Institution

U.S. Army Air Corps pilot takes Air Mail at Marsh Field, California.
Courtesy Smithsonian Institution

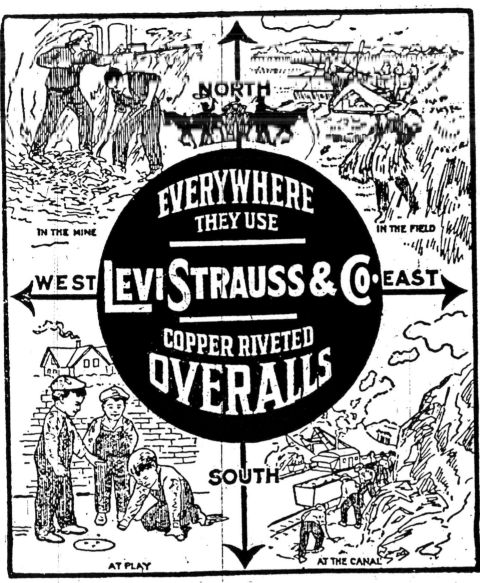

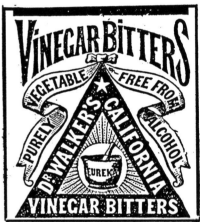
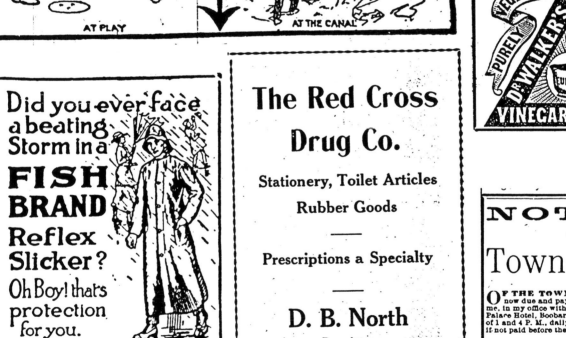

TOWN OF OAKLEY, "R. C. MARSH AND OTHER "SANDLAPPERS"

This is the story of the early development of the barren sand waste lands into what is now a fertile and picturesque area know as Oakley. R. C. Marsh having been one of the first settlers in the area ,and he laid out the town of Oakley, can be called the "Father of Oakley". In 1897 he bought a quarter section in eastern Contra Costa County, moved there and built a home in early 1898. Other early pioneers of Oakley were James O'Hara, Andrew Walker, A. N. Norcross and B. F. Porter.

In seeking to establish improvements of any new and growing community it takes a strong person to take the initiative and R. C. Marsh was the man to put Oakley on the map. The Sante Fe Railroad was extending their line from San Joaquin Valley to Stockton, Antioch and San Fransisco. The Company decided to have a station between Stockton and Antioch and had made five surveys but no decision had been made as to it's location. A few days after Marsh had moved into his new cabin a surveying party came by his place setting a line of stakes. The surveyors told him that the Santa Fe Line would run though his property and he would have to move his house.

The railroad had picked G. W. Knight's ranch ("Knightson"), three and half miles east of the Oakley area because it was the closest to the Southern Pacific Railroad and would likely draw more trade from that area. The station was to named "Meganos". However, when the Santa Fe tried to purchase the right-of-way for their line from Marsh, O'Hara, Walker and Porter, their answer was "No". These leaders said..."No, gentlemen, we will not sell you a right-a-way across the N.W. quarter of section 25, but we will give you the land desired if you will sign an agreement to put down at least a half mile of side track, put up a small room for shelter while waiting for trains and build us a station whenever the business justifies it." The agreement was signed and the

"sandlappers" had scored a big victory. The tiny community now had a station and some status.

Before the grading for the railroad was under way, Marsh applied for a post office and this was done successfully. He received the first letter ever mailed to Oakley. It was sent by the Postmaster General at Washington D. C., Sept. 9, 1898 certifying Marsh as postmaster of Oakley. Supplies were sent to the Antioch post office for the Oakley office and Marsh opened it on Nov. 1, 1898. The first eight months of mail service arrived to and from Antioch by horse and cart. The cart was driven A. N. Norcross and Daniel Methven and the members of the community would donate an occasional coin to buy feed for the horse. In March 1899, the U. S. Postal Service had a notice in the Ledger accepting bids to deliver the mail seven miles to and from Antioch and Oakley six days a week except Sunday. The Ledger said the people in the sand country deserved to get daily mail. After eight months the Postal Service sent the mail from Brentwood to Oakley. The Santa Fe Railroad sent their first train through Oakley on July 1, 1900. Marsh was ready for it and he received and dispatched mail by train for the first time in Oakley's history.

In 1897, James O'Hara put a section of land on the market for $50 an acre and sold all of it in two years. This so-called orchard land was quite sandy and in the early days was a haven for jack-rabbits and coyotes. The people with the courage to locate on the land were called "sandlappers". Almond orchards were planted and, later when fruit trees were introduced, the jack-rabbits and coyotes were the bane of the growers. The "sandlappers" were serenaded at night by the silver tongued coyotes. James O'Hara was the biggest real estate dealer in the Oakley area and was the pioneer and father of the fruit and almond industry of Oakley. He was sometimes referred as the "Father of Oakley" but that is not true. The honor is R. C. Marsh's.

Marsh bought a flat-iron shaped corner of land from Porter and Walker. He offered J. A. Jesse the best lot in that piece of land if he would build a general store equipped with a stock of groceries. When the store was completed, Marsh moved the Post office building on another part of the property and the town of Oakley was started. Shortly after that, he and A. N. Norcross bought 19 acres across the road from the flat-iron property. They platted and recorded it and the town of Oakley was on the map. Substantial concessions were next made to J. M. Augusto to open a blacksmith's shop. Several lots were sold to Brentwood people and a saloon was built. When Marsh platted the map of Oakley, he used the letters of his name for the first letters of the street names, Main, Acme, Ruby, Star, Home and the cross streets were 1st, 2nd, 3rd, 4th and 5th Streets.

The boom was on and by 1905 there were quite a number of "sandlappers" in Oakley and the populace decided to put on a Fourth of July celebration with a jack-rabbit barbecue dinner. When the rest of the county heard of their plans it was thought a big joke, however, the "sandlappers" had the last laugh. The celebration was a huge success even though the temperature was 110 degrees. Washington, D. C. furnished a national flag and pole, an orator came from Stockton, a quartet of singers from Antioch and there were local rhymesters so there was plenty of entertainment for the event. Also the Antioch Band in their white duck suits with red, white and blue ties played special and patriotic music. R. C. Marsh read his original poem, "An Ode to Oakley".

Before the day was over they ran out of the 1500 gift fans as there was approximately 2000 participants at the celebration. By one o'clock 30 gallons of ice cream had been eaten and one stand had sold $85 of soda water alone. In the afternoon, there were races and games of all kinds and prizes for everyone. Later the picnic baskets were opened by the crowd and their contents enjoyed under the oak trees. The celebration concluded with a Grand Ball in the evening with music provided by the Keeney Orchestra from Antioch.

In 1910, James O'Hara added 16 acres to the town site on the east side of Oakley and R. C. Marsh had added a large edition known as "Nob Hill".

Oakley, by 1915, had grown into a good sized town with four churches, two halls for social and club entertainment, a three room school, a 50 member Farmer's Club and a Ladies' Oakley Improvement Club with about thirty members. The post office now had a rural route serving 120 families and a hotel had been built. The Miller-Cummings Company had an asparagus packing plant in Oakley, one of many packing sheds built by the many fruit and vegetable wholesalers on the north side of the Santa Fe tracks. Tomatoes, celery, asparagus, wine grapes and almonds were shipped from Oakley by the carloads to all parts of the country.

Chinese coolies were used for stoop labor in the fields of the large farms and they did the planting, cultivating and harvesting of the crops. Oakley had a Chinatown although a much smaller one than Antioch's. There were several Chinese gambling and opium dens on Ruby Street and the Oakley Hotel was a house of ill-repute.

G. Continente of Pittsburg in 1915 bought 600 acres in the Oakley district and developed it into one of the largest vineyards in the county. He became known as a major grower, shipper and buyer of wine grapes. He also operated a packing shed along the railroad in Oakley.

The early founders of Oakley were men of vision and hard working persons who with determination built the tiny town into a vigorous community of 16,000 by 1991. R. C. Marsh was one of them. He was born in 1838 in Ohio. His first name was Randolph although

110

he never used it in any of his business dealings and, as far as it is known, no one ever called him Randolph. He farmed in Ohio until outbreak of the Civil War, when he enlisted April 1861. He served three months and reenlisted twice for three years service and was mustered out in 1865. He continued farming for a year and then moved to Kansas. After six years he moved to California and settled in Petaluma for three years. Next, he bought land in Lake County and remained there thirteen years before moving to Contra Costa County and being instrumental in forming the town of Oakley. Marsh had three children, daughter "Anna" by his first wife, daughter "Kattie C." and son "Bryon R." by his second wife. (Wives names unknown) He was the first postmaster and held that position for fourteen years, served on the Oakley School Board and was a member of the Oakley Town Board. R. C. was a great booster of the town and aided in many ways in the building of the community and surrounding country. He was a tall slender man with a goatee and was known as a kind and polite gentleman. Marsh loved music and dancing and was often induced to "call off" for the quadrilles when those dances were popular. R. C. Marsh was no relation of John Marsh of the Rancho Los Meganos.

James O'Hara, one of Oakley's founding fathers, gave the town a good start by showing how to grow and cultivate orchards on sand land covered with chaparral and live oaks. Settlers who lived in the adjoining areas said he was crazy if he thought he could grow anything in the sand. However, O'Hara felt differently and bought a section of railroad grant land for $5.00 per acre and with determination and energy turned the barren land into rich and productive orchards. He sold his original section of land for $50.00 an acre and this started him on the way to being a very wealthy man. O'Hara's ranch contained 700 acres with 300 of them in orchards

growing almonds, peaches, prunes, apricots and cherries. He had a large fruit drying plant and large storehouses. O'Hara sold over 4,000 acres of orchards and the reclamation of the sandy land around Oakley added $1,000,000 to the taxable property on the Contra Costa County tax rolls and gave employment to thousands of people. First Street was renamed O'Hara Avenue in his honor.

Among other leaders of Oakley during the early days was S. Dal Porto who built the first hotel and a town hall. Another was Andrew Walker who had purchased 400 acres of swamp land in 1873 near where Oakley is now located. He cleared the land of the chaparral and raised large crops of grain, alfalfa and hay. He sold 900 acres of land he had acquired in 1887 to B. F. Porter. He continued to run his 400 acre ranch until 1905 when he sold it to the California Canner's association. He died in 1906. A. N. Norcross was also one of the pioneers, he settled in the sandland section in 1890. He and Marsh were business partners who severed their business relations after laying out the town. Norcross gave half a block of his property for a school and playgrounds and two lots for the Methodist Church. He was a lover of good horses and always owned the best. His tombstone in the Antioch Oak Grove Cemetery has a beautiful horse engraved on it.

These are a few of the pioneers that started Oakley on it's way to being one of East Conta Costa County's communities.

111

S. Del Porto's Oakley Hotel built prior to 1905. From Author's Collection

Main Street in Oakley looking west. Cira 1905. From Author's Collection

Oakley Sante Fe Railroad Station. From Author's Collection

James O'Hara's home on First Street. From Author's Collection

The Antioch Band that played for the Grand Celebration.

115

First Street in Oakley, later renamed O'Hara Avenue.
From Author's Collection

116

HENRY FULLER BEEDE, A GREAT CITIZEN

This remarkable man descended from an equally remarkable family that had it's roots in France. A record book in fine Spencerian handwriting and still in the Beede family chronicles of the family history. It was written by Thomas Beede, the great grandfather of Henry Fuller Beede, approximately in the late 1780s or early 1800s.

The progenitor of the family was Eli Beede who came from the French island of Jersey in 1705. He was 14 years at that time. His desire to see the New World was intense and he beseeched mother to let him travel to this continent so he could verify the many stories he had heard. His father, a sea captain, had been lost at sea and his mother feared for his life if he undertook the ocean voyage. She finally gave in to Eli's desire and allowed him to make the journey with his uncle, also a sea captain, who was sailing to the New World. The voyage was a disaster for young Eli as he became so seasick for the entire trip and so deathly ill that he refused to return home.

His Uncle had to make provisions for young Eli to stay in the colonies. He was unable to speak or write English and was indentured for 7 years to a farmer named Shaw in the town of Hampton, Mass. At the age of 21 he selected farming as his life work and settled at Kingston, N. H. He married a Miss Sleeper and they had 4 sons and 2 daughters.

Eli was considered a strict but fair man, an honest man, a good neighbor and a sincere Christian. He had a limited education but he could read the Bible and keep the accounts for the large estate he had accumulated. He died in 1784 at the age of 91. The strangest thing about his life was the fact that he never received a letter from, nor wrote a letter to his mother from the time he sailed from the Island of Jersey.

Those following Eli Beede in descent were Thomas Beede, another Thomas Beede, writer, scholar, mathematician, draftsman and a member of Dartmouth College for many years. A third Thomas Beede owned and operated a stage line in Maine. He came to Stockton, Ca., where he operated a livery stable from 1851 to 1853, then went back to Maine and then to Kankakee, Ill. He and his wife moved to Antioch, Ca., and died here. This was Henry Beede's mother and father. This brings it down to Henry Fuller Beede, the fifth in line of descent.

Henry Fuller Beede was born at Farmington, Maine on November 16, 1850. When he was a child, his parents migrated to Kankakee, Illinois, where his father started a business. Henry was the youngest of three boys and was educated in the Kankakee Schools. He became a teacher and telegraph operator from which he earned ample money to pay his way to California. He arrived in the year of 1869 by the way of the Panama Canal route. After arriving at San Fransisco, he took passage by steamer to Antioch where his older brother, George, lived.

George was in the mercantile business with George Israel. Their business was known as Beede and Israel and was located in a new brick building on Main Street (now I Street). Henry was employed by his brother's firm as a salesman and accountant. When Beede and Israel dissolved their partnership, Henry went to work for Abbott and Tuttle whose business was located on the corner of Main and Front Streets (now I and the new Riverview Walkway). The empty brick building of the old firm still stands on this corner. In 1869, Abbott and Tuttle was the center of the commercial life of Antioch, housing the Wells-Fargo & Co. Express office, the post office and the only telegraph office in this section of California, and a stationary and drug store business

Soon after his arrival in Antioch, Henry entered the social life of the town and met Miss Margaret Ellen McNulty, a daughter of Judge J. J. McNulty, Justice of Peace and practicing attorney. She would soon make a big change in the life of young Henry Beede.

He later went to work for the Black Diamond Coal Mining Company in the New York Landing office, (Pittsburg). The coal mining business of Mount Diablo was the main business of the area at that time. Henry's abilities were apparent and the company made him chief accountant in their Nortonville office at the coal mines. Margaret McNulty happened to be teaching school in Nortonville and Henry renewed their acquaintance which turned serious. They were married April 14, 1872 at Nortonville. The marriage produced 11 children and lasted 54 years.

The Antioch School District wanted Margaret Beede to teach lower grade school in the town. One of the school trustees, Mr. Jos. Galloway Jr., the son of Captain Joseph Galloway, induced his father to offer Henry the position of accountant. Henry left the Black Diamond Coal Mining Company to go to work for Captain Galloway's lumber company, Galloway and Boobar, and Margaret became a teacher for the school district. The lumber yard was located in the city block that is bounded by G and H Streets and by 2nd Street and the Riverview Walkway. Later Henry returned to Nortonville as manager of the lumberyard's branch yard there.

In 1877, Captain Joseph Galloway either retired or died and it is not clear which was the case. The new firm of Rouse, Forman and Beede bought the lumber yard from the Captain or his son and heir. Henry Beede had told the new buyers he would like to buy in or he would quit and he was allowed to become a partner. From that time Henry was always identified with the lumber business and under his capable management the firm grew to become one of the largest in the state. W. R. Forman retired and sold his interest to J. P. Abbott and the firm became Rouse, Beede and Abbott. Abbott was a partner of the Antioch Ledger and became State Senator in 1886.

The lumber yard was moved in 1883 to it's present location at E and 2nd Streets. The old Grange Hall at that location was remodeled into the offices and store. An interesting note about Henry, he was into physical fitness and turned the upper part of the building into a gymnasium. The dressing room and shower are still in the upper floor of the building.

A huge city block long u-shaped dock was constructed out into the river and it could accommodate 5 to 7 ships loading or unloading their cargoes of lumber. The corral and barn for the horses was west of the office on 2nd street. Just east of the office was the mammoth planing mill where the rough lumber was finished and shipped to other parts of the country.

At first, the lumber was stacked adjacent to the docks but later a big dry storage shed was built across from the office building.

Captain A. M. Simpson bought into the company about 1895 and it was incorporated as the Antioch Lumber Company in 1907. Captain Simpson was a big power in west coast shipping and owned at least 80 vessels, most were lumber schooners, barks and steam schooners. The Antioch Lumber Company then had a steady source of raw lumber.

Henry Beede always took an active part in every question of importance in the history of Antioch. He was a pioneer who was responsible in a large measure for the establishment of the city. Henry was one of the first town trustees (now known as councilmen) and as such did much to establish Antioch's future. He was a local school board member and as a past teacher made sure the children of Antioch got the best education possible. His efforts, in a large part, helped the schools to have the highest scholastic ratings in the county.

Beede donated the first electric light system for the downtown area to replace the gas street lights. The generator was at the lumber yard and the wires stretched on poles to the downtown lights. All this at no cost to the town. He made it possible for the Sante Fe Railroad to run their rails through the town along the riverfront. He and Abbott owned most of the riverfront property and they donated or sold the right-of-way for a very small sum of money to Sante Fe. The railroad made a big difference in the development of Antioch. Although the Southern Railroad was established first, their station was one mile south of town. The Sante Fe was accessible to the canning companies and producer packers. Beede built a warehouse on the waterfront for these companies' use and the result was the shipping of 8000 carloads of fruit and vegetables a year from Antioch. Sante Fe later bought the warehouse from him and built more of them to handle the vast amount of Delta products being shipped from town.

Henry Beede was very active in the social and religious life of the town. He had friends in high places, one was Captain Dollar who founded the Dollar Steamship Line which later became the President Steamship Line. Beede was a stockholder in Dollar's venture.

Henry was one of the founders and principal supporter of the First Congregational Church. He also was a founder and active member of the Antioch Lodge, F. & A. M. and Royal Arch Chapter of Masons. He was one of the founders of the Antioch Bank and president of it. His home was the center of wonderful hospitality for decades according to the Ledger. Christmas and Thanksgiving were special and crowds of people were welcomed at the house, and often 45 people would sit down to sumptuous holiday meals.

The Beede home, 119 Beede Way, was built over hundred years ago. The spacious house which was situated on a hill and surrounded by grazing dairy herds and the family orchards is now in the midst of modern family homes.

Henry Beede could have had a great political future if he had so desired but he was a staunch Antioch partisan and devoted his life to making it a better place to live. He made new homes available to all including the Italian, Greek and Portuguese immigrants living in Prosserville (western part of Antioch) and Pittsburg. He insured these homes from fire and other damage. Every month he would collect the mortgage payments from each of the owners, carrying a black satchel in which he put the money. Young Henry Fuller Beede Jr. often accompanied his grandfather on these trips and he said that at every stop the owners would insist that Beede Sr. have a drink of wine or grappa. Grandfather Beede was often a little tipsy and "walked on eggs" after these trips according to young Henry.

Beede finally bought all the shares of the company from the estates of Abbott and Rouse and the Beede family now owns all the assets of the corporation. The Antioch Lumber Company is the oldest continuous operating company in California. All five of his sons worked in the business and now his grandson is the last of the line working there.

Henry Fuller Beede Sr. died on April 13, 1926 at the age of 76. In tribute, the entire city, offices, every business house and schools closed for his funeral. At the funeral, people of all walks of life gathered, representatives of every nationality, creed and position. Hundreds came from all over California and other parts of the country to pay respects to Henry F. Beede Sr. Antioch had lost one of her earliest pioneers, a community leader and builder, friend, counselor and most respected citizen.

. Henry Fuller Beede, a great citizen. From Beede Collection

Front row..W. W .Belshaw, Bee McNulty, Olive Beede. Arba Joshlin
Back...Ralph Beede. Swimming party.   From Beede Collection

Henry Beede and part of his family on a picnic. From Beede Collection

Roy, Ralph, Frank, Harry, and Charles Beede with father, Henry F. Beede
From Beede collection

Antioch Lumber Company, 1884, Corner E and 2nd Streets.
From Beede Collection

What Every Woman Should Know

A HOME-MADE clothes sprinkler that will materially lessen the labor of sprinkling clothes is easily made from a quart fruit jar which has a metal screw top lined with porcelain. Remove the porcelain, and with an awl make six small holes in a circle, in the metal top. Fill the jar with water and screw on the top, using the rubber ring to prevent leaking at the side. This method will be found a great time saver.

A WOMAN, whose reputation as a careful and efficient homemaker is widespread, says that one of the most valuable things she has ever discovered for women who do their own work is to use Tuesday for a washday instead of Monday. This woman reserves Monday for cleaning up the house after Sunday, looking over soiled clothing and mending it before it is washed. Moreover, and this is an important reason, when Tuesday is the washday, Sunday evening will not be spoiled by worrying over the coming laundry, putting the clothes to soak and other advance details that washday necessitates.

What Every Woman Should Know

AN apple corer is not generally regarded as a garden tool, but it may be used to very good advantage in planting bulbs. Press the sharp end of the corer into the earth to the desired depth and after removing it, insert the bulb in the hole, replacing as much of the earth as possible. Make several holes close together for larger bulbs. No unsightly marks will thus appear on the lawn.

WHEN baking bread or pastry or roasting meats, the necessity of opening the oven door to observe its progress is a great trial to the cook. The rush of heat is most annoying and sometimes light pastry is spoiled by the jarring of the oven door in closing. One of the greatest conveniences is a glass door such as is attached to the New Perfection Steel Oven. No opening and closing of the oven door are necessary, as one glance will suffice to tell the progress of the baking.

OAKLAND, ANTIOCH AND EASTERN RAILROAD

The Oakland, Antioch and Eastern Railroad could teach Bay Area Rapid Transit a lesson. This pioneer electrified commuter line ran from San Fransisco to Sacramento as part of the Sacramento - Northern Railroad, one of the nation's longest " three rail " electrified lines.

The Sacramento-Northern rail tracks that ran from Sacramento to Chipps Island (across from the Sacramento River at McAvoy's Harbor) were completed in the early part of 1913. The electric trains were put on a ferry boat and sailed across the river to the Pittsburg area west of the P G & E plant where the ferry slip was located. The wooden ferryboat "Bridget" was built in San Fransisco to handle the trains. It was destroyed by fire in June 1913. A contract was let by the O A & E Railway Company to replace the "Bridget" with a steel ferryboat to be built in Pittsburg by the Johnson & Lanteri Shipyard, The steel to be furnished by the new steel-rolling plant in that city.

An article in the Pittsburg-Post Dispatch of 1914 told of an accident during the construction of the steel ferryboat... "Accident Attends Launching. Massive Hull of Ferryboat Falls to Earth. River Embankment Gives Way Under Tremendous Weight Before Craft Reaches Water... A serious mishap befell the steel hull of the new ferryboat being constructed here for the Oakland, Antioch and Eastern Railway when during the process of launching the boat on Thursday afternoon the trestle supporting the ways collapsed, permitting the massive structure to bury itself in the loose formation of earth at the water's edge with the falling force of it's own weight." During the construction of the new ferryboat "Ramona" a contract was let with the Lauritzen Transportation Company of Antioch to provide the transfer of passengers to and from the Pittsburg side of the river and Mallard landing on Chipps Island. They were also using their vessel

"The Duchess" to bring passengers to and from other river towns thereby increasing the ridership of the O A & E. After "Ramona" was relaunched and finished, it was in service until the Railway ceased operations in 1941.

The railway planned a bridge from Mallard on Chipps Island to West Pittsburg. Although sounding and testing was done the bridge never materialized.

The remains of the piling for the slips can still be seen today. The ferry slips were 1,200 feet long and of a sufficient width to admit a standard three-track ferryboat.

For the electric trains to reach the rail junction at Ambrose (west of Pittsburg) a subway had to be built under the Southern Pacific and Sante Fe Railroad's tracks.

A fire destroyed a pile driver belonging to the construction company, the Merury - Elwood Co., but the work proceeded nicely. In the meantime the railroad was completed from Bay Point (Port Chicago) to Oakland in April 1913. A tunnel was built through Redwood Peak at Shepard's Canyon (south of the Caldecott Tunnel). Crews worked from both ends of the tunnel, one from the Contra Costa side and the second crew from Dingee's Ranch. They finally broke through at 10 o'- clock on a Saturday night and shook hands through the gap made by the pickaxes of Sapho Andronike and Nestor Maphtaly, two Greek tunnelmen. The crews met in the center of the 3,400 foot tunnel. The calculations of the engineers was so accurate that the outer circumference of the two bores met within one inch.

The railroad was 29 miles long from Bay Point to Oakland and in the first week of April 1913 the railroad company hosted a trip for the Contra Costa Board of Supervisors on that part of the line. A special car was used to show the progress made in the construction and equipment of the new line of road. Regular service on the road started on April 7, 1913. Here is what the Pittsbug-Post

Dispatch wrote..." It was an interesting trip on Saturday, revealing many wonderful sights to the observant passengers and unfolding an untold tale of life and activity which are sure to follow closely upon the opening of the Oakland, Antioch and Eastern Railroad. Leaving Bay Point the road leads through the towns of Concord, Walnut Creek, Lafayette, passing through the well-known Moraga Grant and then entering the historic redwood canyon. Emerging from this scene of wonderland, where the rugged mountain peaks rise above chasms of abysmal depths on either side the beautiful canyon, which nature evidently designed for a vast park, the line of road enters Oakland by the way of 40th Street and Shaftner Avenue...

Opportunities are golden throughout this territory, and there is already a noticeable stir among prospective buyers of lands and settlers along the road...

The Oakland, Antioch and Eastern Railroad taps a most interesting section of the country. The line will be a tremendous feeder for Oakland besides affording opportunities for obtaining most desirable sites for suburban residences.

The Oakland, Antioch and Eastern Railroad is destined to be come famous for it's usefulness, and it is today, considered one of the most important lines of railroad in Central California."

The connection from Sacramento--Northern and the O A & E was made on July 4, 1913. The Railway Co. officials and a bank officer made an inspection trip over the new line from Sacramento to Oakland, making the trip in 2½ hours.

Twenty new passenger cars and two new engines developing 1,200 horsepower were enroute to the company to increase the size of the rolling equipment.

On Aug. 5, 1983, the O A & E was extended to Railroad Avenue in Pittsburg and this was to be the most eastern terminal. The line never reached Antioch as originally planned. On Aug. 5th, the first train from Pittsburg to Oakland and San Fransisco left in the morning, marking the opening of regular service at 6:30 A.M. The right of way ran through the middle of Eighth Street ending at a small station and freight building on Railroad Avenue.

In 1914, the A O & E merged with the San Ramon Valley Railway, strengthening it's financial position.

The Oakland, Antioch and Eastern Railroad was very successful, operating efficiently and relatively trouble-free from 1913 until 1941 when passenger service ended because of declining ridership. Freight service continued for a while longer.

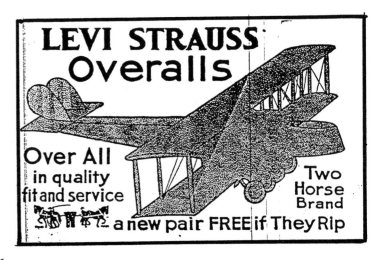

Oakland, Antioch and Eastern Electric Train rounding a curve. Charles Bohakel Jr. Collection

O A & E Ferry, Ramona, carrying railroad cars, 1914. San Fransisco Maritime Museum Collection

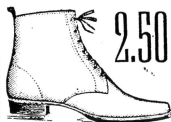

ELECTRIC TRAINS.
On Line of Oakland, Antioch and Eastern Railway.

Courtesy of Contra Costa County History Center.

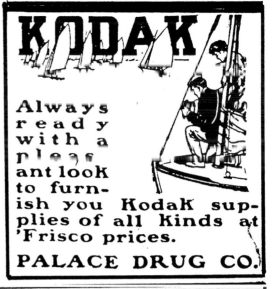

O A & E Advertising Billboards. Courtesy Contra Costa County History Center.

O A & E Freight Engine. Courtesy Charles Bohakel Jr.

O A & E Passenger Train with freight cars at Pittsburg, Courtesy Charles Bohakel Jr.

O A & E Pittsburg Station at Railroad Ave. and 8th St. Courtesy Charles Bohakel Jr.

133

A TYPICAL TEXAS RANGER.

Although Antioch was founded in 1849 by Reverend William Wiggens Smith and his brother, Joseph also a reverend, it wasn't until the year 1865 that the community's first Sunday school was organized that started the various churches. Joseph died shortly after he and his brother founded Antioch. However, William held prayer meetings, baptized and married persons of the community.

The first Sunday school was started by three women, Mrs. William Wiggens Smith, Mrs. Judge Stinchfield and Mrs. M. H. Boothby. They held a meeting to devise ways and means, and decided to ask for subscriptions for the purpose of renting a hall, buying books and papers.

They sent their three young sons, Charlie Smith, Eddie Stinchfield and Hanson Boothby, out to solicit funds. Hanson was the go-getter of the three. He asked for donations from everyone- ...sheep herders, cattlemen, coal miners, store keepers, gamblers, deck-hands, saloon owners, Chinese, Mexicans, Indians and strangers. The following excerpt is from the Ledger..."The first man Hanson met was Major Turner..."Say, Maje, Maw an' the rest o' the women are going to start a Sunday school; and won't you please give something toward buying books and papers ?" The Major reached down in his pocket, took out a dollar and gave it to the boy. Then he led the youth into Frank Williams' saloon and called out to the crowd..."See here, boys, the women are trying to start a Sunday school. Dig up ! Here, Frank Williams, you've children of your own: give this boy a dollar. Here Remfree, I want a dollar toward this Sunday school business. Here John, give us a dollar. (brother John gave two dollars, by the way.) Come on, Al Brink; give us a dollar. Here Paddy McNamee, wake up ! uno peso, muy pronto."

Hanson left the saloon with more than eight dollars. The Major told him to go to every store in town and show up at Dahnken's Saloon on the wharf when the steamer came in and "Hit everybody". The boy followed his instructions but didn't do so well on the wharf. Everyone was in a hurry to disembark from the vessel but he did get a quarter from one passenger. A Captain Thompson, who owned a scow carrying coal from the mines to San Fransisco, gave him two dollars. The same Captain Thompson later gave quite a sum of money to the Congregational Church.

The other two boys collected good amounts of money and the Town Hall was rented, books and papers purchased. The Town Hall was located in the upper story of a building adjoining Dahnken's Saloon on the wharf. That started the first Sunday school in Antioch which was named "Union Congregational Sunday School" because of all the different sects that attended the school. The first teachers were Mrs. W. W. Smith, Mrs. Stinchfield, Mrs. Boothby, Drusilla Boobar and Amelia Kimball.

This Sunday school was the forerunner of Antioch's first church, the First Congregational. On June 12, 1865, a meeting was held in the school house for all those interested in forming a church. The constitution and board members were accepted September 1865. The members were Joseph Galloway, David Woodruff, G. W. Brown, Captain Kimball and William Utter. (all prominent Antioch citizens) The first resident pastor was Reverend C. Morgan in 1865 and his salary was $1000.00 per year. The church was incorporated in 1875.

The Congregational Church building was erected and dedicated May 16, 1869. The original church was torn down and a new building was erected at the southeast corner of Utter and Kimball Streets (6th and F streets) in 1891. This is the oldest church building in Antioch. A 40 foot spire atop the belfry had to be removed because it was severely weakened by the 1906 earthquake. The church bell was cast with 30 silver dollars included in the bell's metal and it was claimed this was the reason it was the sweetest sounding bell in Antioch. This bell is now hung in the courtyard of the present location of the Congregational Church at 620 East Tregallas Road. The 1891 church building and parsonage is now occupied by the Living Word Church.

All the early Protestant denominations originated from the parent organization, the Congregational Church. The Advent Christian Church was organized by Mrs. M. S. Clark, an evangelist of that denomination. It had a membership of about 30, most who were previous members of the Congregational Church. Among these 30 were John Schott, T. N. Wills, Henry Beede, and Dr. E. L. Wemple. Their first resident pastor was Reverend W. R. Young after Mrs. Clark. The Advent Christian church was located at the corner of 4th and I Streets. By 1920, the church was completely disbanded and it's members joined other churches.

The next Protestant church was the Methodist Episcopal Church of Antioch organized in 1889. The principal figures in the movement being Judge J. P. Abott and DR. W. S. George. The first meeting was held in the old Homberg Hall which was located on the site of the future Santa Fe Railroad Station at 2nd and 1st Sts. Those present at this meeting hired Rev. James Blackledge as their first pastor.

The Methodist State Conference sent Reverend Dr. Brill to help in the completion of the organization and trustees. Dr. Brill started a vigorous successful campaign to raise money for a church building and site. Four lots were purchased at the northeast corner of 6th and G Streets. The church was erected on the corner facing G Street with a parsonage facing 6th Street. The cost was $4,878 and it was dedicated on Feb. 8, 1891. There was a fire in 1930 and the church was moved by a crew of Ferd Stamm's to it's present location facing 6th Street. The old church building is now known as the Lombardi Building and has several businesses located in it.

The Church of Christ Scientist members began services at one of their members in 1910. They rented the Union Hall at 3rd and H Streets for their services when they organized in 1911. They bought a lot at the southwest corner of 5th And D Streets in 1912 and a chapel building was built in 1915. This structure was rebuilt and redecorated facing D Street and is still the chapel of the Christian Science Church and Reading Room.

The Catholic Church has always been an important religious institution of Antioch. In 1872, Reverend Father Vincent Vinzes of Bencia was called to the Empire mine to attend to a seriously injured miner. Father Vinezes called the persons of Catholic faith together and celebrated Mass in the home of John Mulhare located a short distance west of Antioch. For more than a year, regular services were held at the Mulhare home. In 1873, a church was built on property located between G and H streets and the building faced 7th Street. The land was donated by L. L. Robinson who owned the Los Medanos Grant. Father Patrick Calahan in 1875 became the first resident priest and a rectory in 1880 was built for his home. He died in 1902 and was replaced by Reverend Father Antone Riley.

In 1905, a beautiful new church was built on the church property to replace the old church. The building was of white sandstone brick, designed and built in the Romanesque style of architecture. The cost was $25,000.-00. This church building was eventually demolished and the property is now a Senior Citizen Complex for elderly persons.

The Holy Rosary Catholic Church is now located on A Street in a large complex of church buildings including a Parochial School.

These five churches were the advance group of the many churches that are now a part of the life of East County.

FIRST CONGREGATIONAL CHURCH

J. C. Bolster, Ph. D., Pastor

Sunday School, 10 A. M.   Preaching, 11 A. M.
Subject:

"Dante's Staircase From Despair to Hope"

Christian Endeavor, 6:30   Evening Sermon 7:30
Subject:

"Eve's Dialogue With the Devil"

Popular subjects given, straight from the shoulder, no sleeping in the pews; every man's opinion courteously regarded, our theology: Not Name or Creed but DEEDS. Stirring music at every service.

This Church will make you welcome.

First Congregational Church built 1869 at Antioch. Rebuilt in 1891. 40 foot spire removed after damage from 1906 earthquake.

Antioch Holy Rosary Catholic Church under construction in 1906. Location on corner of G and H Streets. Site now a Senior Citizen Housing Complex.

Oakley Methodist Church on O'Hare Street. Built approximately 1895.

Antioch Holy Rosary Catholic Church photographed in the 1950's.

Pittburg Congregational Church
in 1913 photograph.

Pittsburg St. Peter's Catholic Church
built in 1914

140

A history of social and fraternal societies is in order. Perhaps no town of similar size in the State of California during it's early history had a better representation of the really worth-while fraternal and social societies than Antioch.

In the early days there was no radio, no television, no drive-in movies and no entertainment to speak of. The town's inhabitants had to provide their own amusements and the social clubs and fraternal societies were the source of the fun amenities. The clubs put on dances, parties, balls, picnics, trips to parks and out-of-town baseball games and they put on plays at the Belshaw Theater. All this besides their basic rules and regulations.

Secret societies were invaluable assets to the community in that their members rarely became public charges and cases of distress of every sort received prompt relief from the lodge or club. They also contributed greatly to the social life of the community, promoting friendship and unity of purpose. While the lodges and clubs were not substitutes for churches, they had many aims and hopes in common. Antioch had many of these benevolent societies whose acts of charity and kindness was well documented. Their goal was to improve the character of man...making him a better citizen, neighbor and friend.

The first permanent fraternal society organized in Antioch was the Masonic Lodge of which there were fifteen charter members. Antioch Lodge No.175, F and A. M. was started June 15, 1865. Two of the charter members were James McNulty, one of Antioch's first lawyers, and Roswell B. Hard, the first mayor and builder of the Hard House on 2nd Street.

The San Joaquin Lodge No.151 of the Independent Order of Odd Fellows was the second oldest lodge in town and was organized January 9, 1869. They only had 5 charter members but soon had 140 members and was one of the largest and most important in

Contra Costa County. This Lodge and the Masonic Lodge jointly owned the building known as the Union Hall at the southeast corner of Third and H Streets. The building still stands at that location.

Ariel Chapter No.42 Order of the Eastern Star was instituted March 30, 1880. This organization started slowly but soon reached 140 members. Their roster included many of the leading citizens of Antioch and the social functions they sponsored were the principal events of the community.

Next was the Antioch Chamber No.65 of the Royal Arch Masons granted an organizational charter June 3, 1884. Among their members was S. H. McKellips, engineer of the Empire Railroad, George Holliday, a remarkable adventurer, and J. P. Abott who became a State senator.

Mizpah Rebeckah Lodge No.102 I.O.O.- F. was organized on June 28, 1888 which soon out grew it's parent lodge, San Joaquin No.151. Many of Antioch's younger set were members and it became a prominent social as well as a fraternal society of the town.

Antioch Encampment No.114 I.O.O.F. consisted of members of the San Joaquin and Byron Lodges and was instituted with a charter membership of 23 on Oct. 9, 1908.

Sometime in the early 1000s or 1870s, a lodge of the Order of Good Templars was formed in Antioch. The main purpose of this lodge was to promote temperance and the great numbers of saloons and bars in those days clearly indicated the need for this organization. After a time it languished and was suspended but in later years it was reorganized and became a strong temperance group for awhile. The Woman's Christian Temperance Union took up the fight from the Good Templars and as late as the 1920s were still in existence.

Another society of youths called the Band of Hope (not a secret one) was organized during that era. The membership consisted of boys and girls of 15 years of age and upwards. It soon failed.

The Native Sons of the Golden West, General Winn Parlor No.32, was instituted July 26, 1884. Every year they held a Grand Masque Ball, usually around Thanksgiving, which was the main social event of the year. They also put on an annual amateur theatrical performance, the entire proceeds were donated to the Homeless Children Fund of California. One of the Past Grand Presidents of this lodge was Senator Charles Mortimer Belshaw.

Antioch Aerie No.785, Fraternal Order of Eagles was started Sept. 1, 1904 with a charter membership of 105 and at one time had more than 300 members.

Antioch Lodge No.1512, Loyal Order of Moose was organized by Dr. Worth S. George in February 1915. The lodge held their meetings in the Foresters of America Hall and maintained elegant club rooms over the Bank of Antioch.

Among other fraternal societies that were established in that era were the Foresters of America, Improved Order of Red Men, Pocohantas Council, The Young Men's Institute (a Catholic order), Columbus Association (an Italian fraternity), U.P.P.E.C., U.P.E.C., I.D.E.S., and S.P.R.S.I.. The last four being Portuguese orders.

All these organizations were involved in social events and the Ledger was full of announcements and stories about them. The following stories are from the paper and give a view of Antioch's social life in those days..."The Masquerade Ball"... "Posters will be gotten out in the Ledger office this week for the Grand Masquerade Ball that will be given Thanksgiving Eve, Wednesday, November 28th, in the Antioch Pavilion by General Winn Parlor, No.32, N.S.G.W.. Robert Wall will be floor director and the floor managers F. Danhken Jr., H. W. Heidorn, W. G. Turner, R. P. Campbell, R. J. Trembath, Frank Thomas, W. W. Belshaw, B. W. Campbell and Charles Bullock. The costumer for the occasion will come from San Fransisco. There will be a prize of

$5.00 for the best dressed gent; $5.00 for the best dressed lady; $2.50 for the best sustained character, gent; $2.50 for the best sustained character, lady; $2.50 for the most original character. Supper will be served at the Arlington Hotel." The other story-..."Fear Not the Ghosts...Mizpah Rebekah Lodge has issued invitations to a Sheet and Pillowcase Party, which will be given in the Union Hall this (Friday) evening, October 19th. None but those in costume will be allowed the privileges of the floor after 12 O'clock. If you see anything that looks like a ghost Friday don't be frightened, for it will probably be one of the guests wending his way to the Sheet and Pillowcase Party."

So went the leisurely pace of life that depended on the fraternal orders, societies and clubs that made Antioch's early days interesting and were a great value to the social life of the community, promoting good fellowship and unity of purpose.

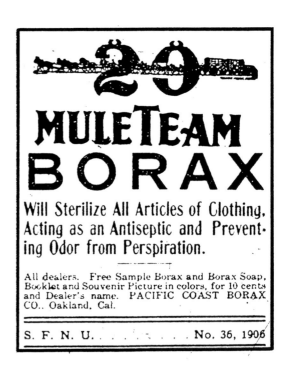

Lodge Directory

ANTIOCH PYRAMID No. 24

Meets Second and Fourth Thursdays
at Masonic Temple.
D. N. STEWART, Toparch.
W. H. WINFREE, Scribe.

ANTIOCH ENCAMPMENT No. 114, I. O. O. F.

Meets the first and third Tuesdays
of each month, in Union Hall, at 8
o'clock p.m.

W. H. Lunny,
Chief Patriarch.

L. A. Stark,
Scribe.

SAN JOAQUIN LODGE, No. 151 I. O. O. F.

Meets on Thursday of
each week at 8 o'clock
p. m., in Union Hall.

H. M. Jensen,
Noble Grand.

H. H. Bruns,
Secretary.

GENERAL WINN PARLOR, No. 32, N. S. G. W.

Meets at 8 o'clock p.m. on the second
and fourth Wednesdays of each month
in Union Hall.

Westley Field,
President.

A. B. Lorber,
Secretary.

ANTIOCH AERIE, 785, F. O. E.

Meets the first and third Wednesday
evenings of each month in Union Hall.
Visiting brothers cordially invited.

Frank Buys,
President.

C. A. Sweeney,
Secretary.

ANTIOCH CHAPTER Order of De Molay

Meets 8 p. m. first and
third Tuesdays of each
month in City Hall Club
Room.

Elvin Adams,
M. C.

D. F. Nelson,
Scribe.

RED MEN BALL SUCCESSFUL

The ball given by Otoe Tribe No.
196, Improved Order of Red Men,
was a decided success, both socially
and financially, and those present
were highly pleased with their entertainment. The music was excellent,
the selections being the latest to be
secured and each number well rendered. Regardless of the card party
at Oakley and a dance at Pittsburg,
there were representatives from Byron, Brentwood, Knightsen, Oakley,
Pittsburg and the surrounding country. It is understood the lodge will
clear about $40.

WILL BEGIN REHEARSING

Antioch's amateurs will commence
rehearsing next week for the annual
play to be given by the Native Sons'
for the benefit of the Homeless Children fund. The piece selected is "Facing the Music." There are three acts
and the second is funnier than the
first and the third more laughable
than the other two, so the audience
is certain to be well pleased. It is
understood the cast will be about
the same as last year.

FIRST SOCIAL

A good crowd was present at the
Pocahontas social in Forester's Hall
Tuesday evening, regardless of the
inclement weather and the hours
proved pleasant for all. A feature
was the singing of Mrs. Gillespie and
piano selections by Miss Bose of
Stockton. Mrs. G. A. Johnson held
high score in playing whist and was
rewarded with a silver mustard cup.
Mrs. Copley was second and received
an ivory powder box. Charles Cooper
won the first prize for gentlemen, a
pair of suspenders, and Mr. Copley
the second, a box of stationery.

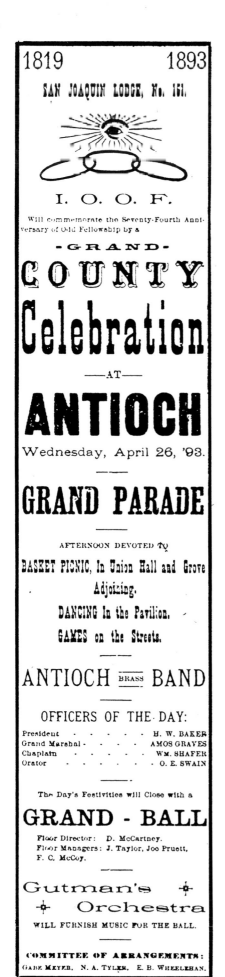

Early East Contra Costa County motorists were enthusiasts. Doctors were the primary buyers of automobiles but the rest of the populace was not far behind.

The purchase of an auto in the early 1900s was front page news and trips by autos were written stories in the newspapers.

The majority of autos in those days were Fords, Chevrolets, Hudsons, Dodges, Buicks and Overlands. Some of the other makes in East Contra Costa County were Page, Studebaker, Mercer, EMF, Maxwell, Saxon, Pope, Reo, Little Giant Truck, White Truck, Mack Truck, Garfield Truck, Cleveland Truck, Vini Delivery, Case, Cadillac, Cole, Grant "6", Mitch "6", Stanley Steamer, Durant, Hupmobile, Gardner and Star. These were just a few of the many makes sold in the county.

At one time in the early history of automobiles there were 2,200 different makes being built. Included in these many autos were 125 steam-powered vehicles. None of the steamers survived and only a few of the gasoline-powered autos are around today.

The automobile photographs are vehicles of the local owners.

Frank Page of Oakley owned a Mitchell Six like this one.

Saxon Touring Auto with top up. C.W Minaker, owner.

Saxon Touring Auto with top down.

1921 Saxon

1920 Saxon

Overland Touring sedan.

Maxwell Touring sedan.

TWO AUTOS PURCHASED

C. W. Minaker, the rancher east of town, took delivery of a Saxon six touring car this week. Mr. Minaker and family are anticipating many pleasant trips with their friends. Frank Miller of Oakley, was the purchaser of a Mitchell six. Mr. Miller has been thinking seriously about purchasing an auto for several years, but did not find one that just suited his fancy until he investigated the Mitchell. His daughters expect to master the art of driving and they are anticipating much pleasure from the many trips planned. Both sales were made by Henry Stearns, agent for these cars in this county.

147

Red Crown 1915 Ford Model T truck delivering Zerolene fuel.

1917 Ford Model T Roadster with young East County couple.

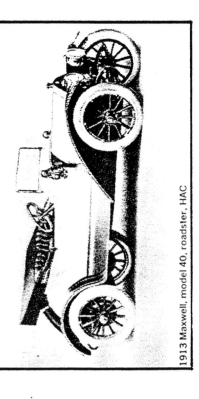

1913 Maxwell, model 40, roadster, HAC

NEW DELIVERY CAR

S. Michelotti, who conducts the Italian Bakery, has just purchased a handsome looking auto delivery wagon. The new car has a cream colored body and presents an attractive appearance. Mr. Michelotti has a splendid trade not only among the Italian people, but Americans as well and is now giving them excellent service.

Chain driven truck with solid rubber tires. Unknown make. Thought to have been owned by concrete tile company in Knightson.

TWELVE CYLINDER PACKARD

C. M. Belshaw arrived here Wednesday from San Francisco in his handsome twelve cylinder, seven passenger Packard car, which he purchased some time ago, making the trip by way of the Franklin Canyon route. The machine is not only striking in appearance, but possesses a wonderful driving equipment, the motor, which is a forty-three horsepower, being considered as near perfection as can be produced and every refinement possible is provided. The Delco system of starting and lighting is a feature, there being a separate indicator for each, as well as for lubricating, and a special thermometer, which gives the temperature of the motor. So smoothly does the engine run it can scarcely be heard and in starting the car moves off without the slightest jar. It is probably the most elaborately finished automobile in Contra Costa County. Mr. Belshaw stated that coming up from San Francisco the car averaged ten miles to the gallon of gasoline, which is very good for such a large machine and also new, while the roads are not in the best condition

Antioch couple with their automobiles, 1925

1939 American-Austin Bantam Roadster. Photographed in Antioch. Owner unknown.

1911 E-M-F, model 30, touring, HAC

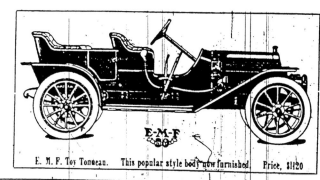

E. M. F. Toy Tonneau. This popular style body now furnished. Price, $1120

Dave Irvin Has New Car

Dave Irvin, bookkeeper of the C. A. Hooper Co., this city, the perennially smiling Dave, is sporting a new four-passenger country club Overland automobile, purchased this week.

And to make things more binding, his father, Dave Gatto, has just completed a fine garage at his home to house the machine. The garage is equipped with electric lights, water faucets, porcelain wash bowl, con-concrete floor and pit. A concrete driveway to the street is to be built.

This ought to be good for a ride, David, old boy. How about it, Oliver?

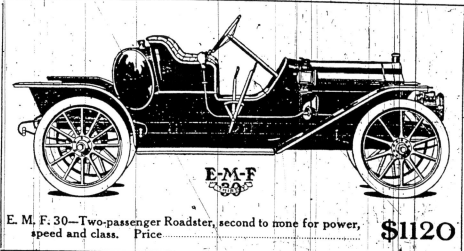

E. M. F. 30—Two-passenger Roadster, second to none for power, speed and class. Price _____ $1120

HAS NEW PEERLESS CAR

"Bob" Love took delivery this week of a handsome Peerless sedan that has been attracting general attention. Mr. Love drove a Peerless "chummy roadster" about a year, using the car in his recent trip to Mexico, but decided recently to secure an enclosed machine.

BOUGHT "GRANT SIX"

Supervisor J. H. Trythall is now traveling in a new automobile, having purchased a "Grant Six" five passenger touring car last week from the Antioch Garage, agents for that auto. It is a classy looking machine and new to this section. However, the agents for the car state that it possesses all the staying qualities of the illustrious general of the same name.

153

1936 Cord Phaeton Convertible. These automobiles
are now desirable collector items. Tom Hodson of
Antioch owned a Cord Automobile.

These four early 1900 era trucks were part of the fleet that were used by
the big Brentwood Farms to bring the field harvest to the packing shed.

1921 Overland Coupe

155

Early race car. Probably a Mercedes-Benz from the looks of the radiator.

Dr. Worth S. George at the wheel of his auto. Decorated for a parade in Antioch.

AN EARLY FIRE DEPARTMENT

Fire was the sleeping monster that terrorized the small towns and villages when it awakened. It usually destroyed everything in it's path until drastic measures were taken to quell it. Sometimes it was put out before it burned out of control.

A fire bell was hung in the first City Hall (a small wooden building), and when there was a fire, the first person that could get there rang the bell alerting the small town of Antioch. Every able-bodied man and boy turned out to fight the fire. This was in 1856.

Many times men who were in the area at the first signs of fire, went into action before help arrived. One man mentioned by the Ledger in 1870 said..."Great credit was due Paul Laventhal who acted so courageously at the fire in the Post Office building on Second Street. He tried three times to mount the top of the roof before he made it and helped put out the fire. He was slightly burned." The Ledger also stated at a later date, that a fire apparatus was needed in an effort to arm the town against a conflagation. It added, if a fire came now, the most they could do would be to sit down and watch it burn. That just about happened a year later.

On August 23, 1871, Antioch was almost consumed by the fire monster. A fire broke out on Main Street (I Street) in a wash house of the Griffin Hotel, southeast corner of Main and Wyatt (2nd and I Streets). It started in the early morning, a violent north wind was blowing, and most persons were asleep. In no time at all the fire spread rapidly. Before Hop Sing's Wash House, in the path of the fire, was torn down and thus stopped the fire, three blocks of the town was leveled by the fire. Eighteen thousand dollars worth of property was destroyed, of which ten thousand was insured. The townspeople had won that at a very expensive cost.

The citizens of the town assembled at National Hall on November 7, 1871, after the disastrous fire, and or-

ganized a fire company to be known as the Antioch Hook and Ladder Company No.1. J. W. Galloway was elected president, M. S. Levy was secretary, G. C. Carman made treasurer. Foreman S. Jessup (same as chief), 1st Assistant Fred Wilkening and 2nd Assistant Daniel Cleaves were all elected for those positions.

The Fire Company was made up entirely of volunteers who paid to join the organization. It was fashionable to join and was, moreover, an exciting time for the men. The Company bought it's equipment with money raised from dances and dues. The Ledger exhorted the citizens to attend these dances and considered it the duty of property owners to buy a ticket whether they attended or not.

The town trustees were well aware of the town's danger from fire and on March 14, 1872 they adopted two ordinances to control fire danger as much as possible. Ordinance No.4 was to protect dwellings and stores from destruction by fire from defective flues, pipes or chimneys. No stove or furnace to be operated without them. The same to extend at least two feet above the roof ridge and be insulated where they went though the roof. The City Marshal inspected these flues, chimneys and pipes every first Monday of April and November. It was considered unlawful for any person to deposit hot ashes in any wooden vessel, or on any vacant lot or premises, unless the same have been thoroughly saturated with water. Failure to comply was subject to a fine not less than $20 nor more than $100, or jail or both.

Ordinance No.5 was a supplement to No.4, it provided a change in the penalty . It gave the offender 10 days to comply with the order to repair or replace any violations of No.4. The fine was $2.50 a day or jail, or both.

On June 3, 1872, a petition was filed by the citizens paying the trustees to purchase the fire apparatus belonging to the Hook and Ladder Com-

157

pany in the amount of cost, not to exceed $150.00. The motion was accepted and a report was made on January 5, 1874. The Antioch Board of Trustees meeting had the report from Mr. Brown, Committee on the state of the fire apparatus... "Report...I find the wagon on the lot of Peter Lane in broken condition and unfit for use, two hooks unfit for use, one ladder used as a fence on the premises of Peter Lane, one ladder on George McCoy's premises, one ladder on the premises of Chase & Robbins (livery stable) with one ladder and three poles on the wagon, all more or less out of repair, and the building was claimed by Mr. Chase for rent of the ground." The Fire Commissioner was told to repair and find a suitable place to store the fire apparatus, also to sell the wagon and building.

The Board of Trustees passed ordinance No.24 on March 1, 1875, establishing a Fire Department governed by a Chief Engineer with First and Second Assistants who were elected to those positions, for one year terms, by the members of the Fire Company. There were provisions made for companies to be formed, to be governed by a fireman and two assistants also to be elected by the members at the same time as the Chief Engineer and his Assistants. The equipment they had at this time, besides the hooks and ladders, was two dozen paper buckets purchased from a San Fransisco firm for $23.00 on January 20, 1874. A used hand operated pumper was bought about that time. The fire department was known as the Antioch Volunteer Fire Company No.1.

The Antioch Fire Company had 16 members in 1875 and many were the towns notable citizens, they paid $2.50 to join the Company.

Antioch Volunteer Fire Company No.1 had 36 volunteers as of April 23, 1881. Among them were Henry Beede and Rouse, owners of the lumber yard, S. B. Joslin, saddle and harness shop, Dahnken, owner of the wharf, McCartney, a store owner, William Remfree, the

proprietor of a barbershop and saloon and many other business men. All were aware of the importance of having an active and energetic fire department. On May 10 1890, a notice that Dr. W. S. George and James Remfree were elected and installed as members. During this period of time, the only pieces of equipment were a hose cart, a hand pumper, and a wagon with short ladders and hooks, all pulled by volunteers. A hook was a pole with an iron hook on one end that could be used to break windows or make holes in roofs.

An account of the Noakes and Hough barn fire was in the Ledger on April 11, 1896. The barn, which contained 150 tons of hay and all their horses and wagons, caught fire. The first volunteers who arrived rushed in the barn to cut loose the horses and save as many as they could. All were saved except one horse who was burned so badly, it was put out of it's misery with a gunshot to the head. While these firemen were at work in the barn, the others arrived with the hand-drawn pumper, hose cart and the wagon with the ladders and hook. The paper said there was a scarcity of water to fight the fire at first but as soon as the valves (leather ones) on the pumper engine got soaked up she threw a pretty good stream. The Noakes and Hough barn was completely destroyed, but the firemen saved the big Chase Livery Stable which was in front of the barn on Main Street (I Street). The barn owners were covered by an $1800.00 insurance policy issued by Henry Beede. The Ledger went on to say Antioch had the best kind of fire workers and it was due to their heroic efforts the town was not burned before this action.

Membership in the Antioch Volunteer Fire Company was usually open to anyone who qualified, but the requirements were tough. The volunteers were, for the most part, big, athletic and robust young men. They had to attend drills and when they became proficient they chose the specialty they were most qualified to perform. To become a ladderman whose work was to vent a burning building from the roof and to carry hoses to roof fires and perform rescues. He had to be agile and sure-footed. To become an engineer and work with pumpers and hydrants, he had to have a knowledge of mechanics and hydraulics. The Chief Engineer was a must for the Fire Company and his assistants were usually plumbers. The hosemen enter the burning building and pour water on the flames and keep doing it until the fire is out. The salvage firemen's job was to protect property and they carried out all the movable items that they could save. The driver of the fire truck (acquired later) was the most important man in the Company. It was his job to get the pumper to the location as soon as possible and as safely as possible. The lives of the firemen riding on the truck was in his hands, he had to maneuver the vehicle so the high pressure hose could be quickly fastened to the fire hydrant, then he could help with the hose.

The comradeship was very close in the Volunteer Fire Department and after their drills they would party and play cards at the Fire house. It was an exclusive club!

In 1902, the town trustees bought a four wheeled wagon. Also 300 feet of 2 inch hose, 4 fire extinguishers of $22\frac{1}{2}$ gallons and 4 of 5 gallons, all to be carried on the wagon. "Old Betsy", the ancient fire pumper was still in operation and had to be hand pulled to fires.

The need for additional fire equip ment was evidenced at the Grammar School fire on G Street in July 1913. The Ledger headlined..."The Fire Yesterday Merely A Case Of Good Luck... Can anyone doubt we need additional fire equipment, after witnessing the spectacular yesterday, when the firemen were battling against heavy odds with inadequate apparatus to save a burning building and endeavoring to keep the fire from spreading. Had the blaze ever secured a good start in the Gram-

mar School building nothing could have stopped it and several blocks of the best residence district of the town would have been laid to waste." The editorial went on to say the paper had been calling attention to the needs of the Fire Department saying the department's ladders wouldn't reach a second story window.

An another editorial talked about the very grave danger of fire to the town when the only pump furnishing water to the town's mains broke down. It asked the people of Antioch to vote for a better water system and more adequate fire protection which would help reduce their fire insurance rates.

The method of fire alarm signals had improved. In the early days, the ringing of the fire bell indicated a fire was burning somewhere in the town limits. Looking for smoke was the only way to find the location. When the town's streets were changed to letters and numbers it was easy to locate fires. The number of gongs of the fire bell or blasts of the paper mill whistle gave the location. The first set of signals would indicate the numbered streets, then the second set would indicate the lettered streets. An example...First set of four signals would be 4th Street, the second set of 5 signals would be E Street (using the following method, 1 signal= A, 2= B, 3= C, 4= D. 5= E so forth) so the fire would be at 4th and E Streets. Fire alarm signal cards were made available free of charge at the Bank of Antioch. People were advised to hang them by their telephones.

Care had be exercised when calling in giving alarms of fire to give correct locations. The Ledger of 1913 said at a recent fire, several different phone calls were sent to the phone office telling of the blaze but only a few were correct. The paper gave the phone number Main 891 as Assistant Fire Chief Azevedo's barber shop for day calls and his residence number Main 1501 for night calls.

In 1913, a new fire bell was purchased by the trustees but Chief Ferd Stamm said it wasn't loud enough to hear at his home at 5th and B Streets. The trustees told the W. T. Garrett Company to come check it out or there would not be a payment for the bell. A new louder bell was installed and, incidentally, Ferd Stamm was chairman of the Board of Trustees. New fire hose, 1200 feet, was bought from the Bowers Rubber Company of Pittsburg, Ca. Again Stamm was instrumental in awarding the contract. Five different bids were submitted, but Bowers got the nod even though theirs wasn't the lowest bid.

By 1915, fire box alarms were installed on strategic street corners. There were six of these alarms with three more established by the Paper Mill near their plant. The Antioch Women's Club gave the money for the automatic fire alarm apparatus that was installed in the fire house.

Hose cart buildings were located at various sites around town and the first volunteers would run the cart to a fire hydrant for a hook-up closest to the fire.

In 1915, the Volunteer Fire Company was reorganized with Ferd Stamm, Chief (he was chief for 27 years starting 1910), Pete Donlon, 1st Assistant Chief and C. W. Keeney as 2nd Assistant Chief. Also at the same time the trustees appointed four of the volunteers as Deputy Town Marshals to serve without pay. The crowds at the fires often shouted unwanted advice which was confusing to the volunteers who had to listen for official commands.

To help pay for the purchase of a 1916 Ford - LaFrance Fire Engine, the firemen held the big Fourth of July Celebration of 1916 under their auspices. This was a huge event and held the parade, for the first time, on paved streets which brought a great number of floats, bands and marchers to Antioch. There were motorcycle races, foot races, motor boat races, horse show, auto show, free barbecue, an exhibition of a new sport called "surf-boarding" and dances. The biggest event was the Fire Department Hose Cart Race with four departments participating, Benicia, Pittsburg, Bowers Rubber Works and Antioch. The course was from 2nd Street to the Grammar School on G Street and Antioch won the race. When the celebration was over the Fire Department netted $236.15.

The next big money making event was the Fireman's Ball on September 22, 1916. No amount of profit was listed, but it must have been enough to make the down payment on the fire truck. Buying the first mechanized piece of equipment, owned by the volunteers, was the Ford - LaFrance combination chemical engine and hose car. It was equipped with a 25 gallon chemical tank with 150 feet of small hose for the tank, a 16 foot extension ladder, two fire extinguishers, and 500 feet of 2½ inch hose in a compartment. All of which was mounted on a 1916 Ford chassis and was purchased on September 26, 1916 at a cost of $1,357.75.

In responding to a first alarm it is imperative to get some men and equipment to the blaze as soon as possible. This chemical truck was probably used for that purpose. It was supplemented by the four wheel hose wagon it towed to the fires. Just several men and a single piece of equipment can stop a blaze early in it's start faster and easier than the whole Company after it has gotten out of control.

The Volunteer Fire Company had trouble making payments of the fire truck and on March 12, 1917 they asked the town trustees for help making the loan payments. This fire truck was discarded in the scrap metal drive of World War II. (Antioch has a habit of tossing away it's history)

The incentive for reorganization of the Volunteer Fire Company was the new 1925 Dodge powered Seagraves Pumper. Bids were accepted Oct. 25, 1925 for a Pumper Engine. Seagraves, Stutz and American-LaFrance Companies put on a demonstration of their pumpers with 750 gallon a minute capacity on October 27th. This day was like a holiday for the town of Antioch and a huge crowd turned out for the tests of four pumpers. Seagraves won the test and the City Council purchased their pumper for $6,500.00.

The result of that purchase created a new department with Ferd Stamm still Chief and Peter Donlon, his Assistant Chief. George Ackerman was elected Secretary to do the "heavy" work when he wasn't wrestling a hose and Treasurer was Ralph Beede. The Department also had seven Fire Policemen used for crowd control. Engine Company No.1 (Seagraves Engine) was headed by Captain Westley Field with fifteen firemen. Engine Company No.2 (Ford-LaFrance Engine) with Captain Charles Hornbeck who had nine firemen. Hose Company No.2 with Captain William Beasley had seventeen firemen. Hose Company No.3 with Captain A. A. Waldie had thirteen firemen and Hose Company No.4 with Captain David Arata had ten firemen.

As mentioned before, many of the town's notable men served in the Volunteer Fire Company. Among them were Joe Cesa, James Donlon, James Taylor, Jas. Carey, Marino Marchio, Ollie Klengel. Frank Rodgers and many others.

Frank A. "Tiny" Rodgers was hired in 1925 by the trustees to drive the Seagraves Engine. He was the first paid part-time fireman of Antioch. Tiny Rodgers was injured in a traffic accident while driving the 1916 Ford-LaFrance Engine on June 14, 1925. He was in the hospital at Oakland for several weeks. The town had to pay his hospital bill plus his regular wages. The total amount came to $832. This triggered the Antioch Firemen's Insurance Policy as the trustees found that the $150.00 a year policy was much cheaper than the $832.00 for one fireman's injury.

Antioch Fire Chief Ferdinand Stamm Jr. was the man that did everything in his power to make the Antioch Fire Department the best possible one in the county. He was Chief for 27 years until his death in 1937 and before he made Chief, he was a volunteer. He was one of Contra Costa County's wealthiest residents and was a self--made man in every sense of the word. His business ability was exceptional, a straight thinking man with a common sense approach to problems, personal or civic. He was a town trustee for nine years and made sure the Fire Department got apparatus when they needed it.

Ferd Stamm pushed through the new high pressure water system which resulted in low fire insurance rates for Antioch. He fought for and secured the 1916 Chemical Truck, the 1925 Seagraves Pumper and the 1934 Van Pelt Pumper for the Fire Department. He served the community for thirty years without payment.

The first rescue squad was started in the early 1930's using "Pull Motors" for resuscitation The firemen were often called to the Antioch Hospital on Sixth Street to administer oxygen.

On the first day of May 1930, the town of Antioch hired two firemen at $125.00 a month for each of them. They were the first full time firemen on the town's payroll and they also had apartments for them and their families to live in at the new City Hall. Charles D. Sweeney (son of Police Chief Charles A. Sweeney and James Taylor were the two men hired. Taylor's little son grew up thinking the red fire engine was their family auto. Charles Sweeney joined the volunteers in 1906 and he held jobs as a telegrapher for Southern Pacific Railroad, projectionist for the Casino Theater and as an electrical contractor. He was promoted to captain in 1933. After seven years James Taylor resigned with the rank of captain. Kingsley Shaw was hired to replace Taylor. John Granganelli was also hired as a relief fireman bringing the total number of paid firemen to three in 1937.

When Chief Ferd Stamm died in 1937,

Peter Donlon Sr. was named Fire Chief and Charles Sweeney as Assistant Chief. At the same time Buss Ackerman and Pat Bogan were promoted to captains, Kingsley Shaw and John Granganelli were made lieutenants.

Rural Fire Protection Ordinance 132A was passed by the City Council in 1937. The City Fire Department would serve a half mile area outside Antioch's boundaries with fire protection for a paid fee from property owners. One luckless home owner whose house was at 12 E. Sixth Street, just outside the city limits, and who hadn't paid a fee, had a fire. The volunteers rushed to the nearest fire hydrant, hooked up and was ready to douse the fire when the Chief arrived and stopped them. The owner hadn't paid the fire fee and the house burned to the ground.

Charles Sweeney became Antioch's first paid Fire Chief in 1942. While serving in that position he was also the city's Building Inspector, Electrical Inspector, Health Inspector and the Zoning Inspector. He was the first fireman to retire in September 1950 after 34 years as a volunteer and paid fireman. For two years after his retirement, he was Chief of the Bethel Island Fire Department.

In 1950, a 1927 Ford pickup truck was donated by R. Houdashelt to the volunteers and they rebuilt it into a fire truck. This truck is still owned by the City of Antioch and it is driven occasionally in parades.

Throughout the turn of the century, fires in Antioch burned a major portion of the business district at one time or another. Most of the dates of these fires are not available, however, the Fiberboard Paper Mill was completely burned to the ground in 1912. The big straw stacks of the mill were continuously catching fire causing great excitement in the Prosserville area of town. Everyone hosed their roofs and the children enjoyed the spectacle. The stack fires sometimes burned for several days. In 1935, the Heath Apartment fire also burned five other apartment buildings.

The fire report of 1937 showed the Department turned out for 80 alarms and three of those were straw stack fires at the paper mill.

Other major fires were the Towne House in 1935, the Sears Warehouse in 1960, in 1961 the Riverview Lodge fire and the Battaglis Banquet Center fire in 1970. Another big fire in that era was the rupture of the high pressure gasoline line on Russell Drive and the flames from the result of the rupture destroyed two homes and damaged two others.

The Riverview Fire District was formed in 1975 combining the Antioch and Pittsburg Fire Departments. On July 1981, the volunteer firemen were phased out of the manpower of the Fire District. Some of the volunteers elected to become department regulars while others retired as volunteers.

The volunteer's work was over and they had accomplished miracles in keeping Antioch from being devastated by the fire monster.

FIRE ALARM SIGNALS

LOCATION OF BOXES

Box	Location
No. 5	First and L
No. 7	Fourth and K
No. 9	Second and H
No. 12	Fifth and G
No. 14	Sixth and F
No. 16	Fourth and C
No. 18	Third and G
No. 21	Eighth and D
No. 24	Sixth and C
No. 26	Eighth and F

Nos. 41, 42, 43, 112, located on Paraffine Co.'s Property.

Ferd Stamm (standing on top of cart with tie) was the
Antioch Volunteer Fire Chief for 27 years.

Photo of Antioch Crack Hose Team of '06 Shown

Found among a collection of historical pictures, one of the Antioch Crack Hose Team, was brought to The Ledger yesterday by Carl Keeney. The photograph, well preserved, is of the team taken July 4, 1906, following the establishing of a record of 54 seconds to run 300 yards and make hose connection.

The personnel of the team was: Γ. A. Donlon, Ferd Stamm, Jas. D. Donlon, Jack Courtney, George Upton, Paul Owens, Jack Healey, Harry Woolcott, Charles Bullock, F. L. Furbee, Jack Skeels, Charles Wall, Henry Taylor, Ralph Smith.

The record was established as part of the July Fourth observation in Antioch. The following year Martinez eclipsed Antioch by 5-8 of a second.

The photo is on display in The Ledger window where it may be viewed for a time.

Charles D. Sweeney, one of Antioch's first paid fireman and the first paid Fire Chief. 1916–1950
Courtesy of Riverside Fire District

The original written contract for the 1916 American La France Ford fire engine.
Courtesy of Riverside Fire District

American La France Ford with two unknown firemen. Fire Department was located inside the back of Antioch City Hall. Courtesy Riverside Fire District

1925 Seagraves pumper fire truck with volunteer firemen. Frank "Tiny" Rodgers (paid fireman) is behind the wheel. Police Chief Sweeney on the right
Courtesy of Riverside Fire District

1927 Ford donated by R. Houdashelt and made into a fire truck by the volunteer firemen. The truck is still owned by the City of Antioch and used in parades.
From Author's Collection

166

ANTIOCH AND PITTSBURG HAD THEIR SHARE OF PROSTITUTION AND GAMBLING

Antioch and Pittsburg had more than their share of gambling and prosti-tution. Prostitution is the practice of submitting to sexual intercourse for pay. It is sometimes referred to as "the oldest profession" and can be traced to the earliest recorded times. In Egypt and Asia Minor, several centuries before Christ, it was a part of certain religions. Rome taxed and registered prostitutes. In the Middle Ages, they were licensed and regulated by law. In the Near East, North Africa and most Asian countries, prostitution is generally an accepted institution.

Various attempts have been made during the past centuries to control and solve the problem of prostitution. No method has succeeded and it continues to exist. Today it continues to be a problem for physical, mental and moral health. States and communities, in this country, have had laws against prostitution for many years but toleration or "legal looking aside" has often co-existed with these laws. Suppression of prostitution was ineffective but, from time to time, police were forced by public opinion to raid the public brothels. In the 1800s, Contra Costa County's law officials and judges were known to bend the law to the highest bidder.

Two laws that had an effect on prostitution was the Red Light Abatement Law which made places used for illegal gambling , prostitution or bathhouses declared nuisances. An order of abatement and a judgment or fine is made against the operators and/or owner of the declared nuisance buildings. A lien could be placed on the property, fixtures, movable property and other items. Usually a fine was levied consisting of the year's rental of the building and it's closure for one year and the sale of all the interior movable property. The other law was the White-Slave Act of 1910 (often called the Mann Act) which outlawed transporting a woman across a state line for immoral purposes.

Prostitution in Antioch and Pittsburg from 1870 until 1919 was made very profitable by the coal miners, cowboys, riverboat men, soldiers and farm hands in the area. On Saturday nights, these men made their first stop at the local barbershops where they got a shave, haircut, a hot bath and a change of clothes. Avalzedos' Barbershop located on Second Street in Antioch had three bath tubs and was the agent for the Stockton Laundry. His was a popular shop. After these preparations, the men were ready for a night on the town.

On Saturday night, or any night, there were plenty of attractions, legal and illegal, in Pittsburg and Antioch. Many gambling places, saloons, houses and arks of prostitution prevailed in and near both towns. Saloons and brothels outnumbered any of the other businesses located in these two communities. Tyler's Hotel in Antioch was called the "Bucket of Blood" because of the bloody, unconscious bodies sometimes found in back of the hotel on Sunday mornings. The "ladies of the night" at the hotel had rough partners and fights occurred between the hotel bar's customers. In 1918, a man was killed at that location which was then owned by Al Ross. Raymond Unconetti was thrown over a railing of a stairway after being hit on the head with a club or bottle by Ross. Unconnetti's neck was broken and he laid on the ground for hours before help arrived. He gave a dying statement to Dr. W. S. George and Ross was arrested.

There were houses of ill-repute on Sherman Island, floating scows and arks, usually two tied together with one used as a dance hall and the other with cribs for the prostitutes, anchored on the river across from Antioch. The arks were houseboats of their era, without power and towed to their locations by the scows or powerboats. The arks had tiny rooms and some even had outhouses attached to the vessel. They looked like oblong boxes sitting on barge-like hulls.

The dancehall scows looked much like the arks but were equipped with a mast and large sail and were able to tow the "arks" if necessary.

Just west of Antioch's Public Wharf, houseboats were tied up to the shore, also houses on pilings. To reach them, one had to traverse narrow wooden walkaways over marsh, tules and water at high tide. Many a tipsy customer had his ardor cooled when he tumbled off the walkaways into the mud or water.

Among Antioch's many brothels was Ethel Anderson's on the corner of 3rd and K Streets, Turner and Danken's Hotel that was over the Shanghia Cafe at 2nd and I Streets, one was above the old French Laundry on 2nd Street and the old Pitt House, also known as the Hartman House, located at the corner of 2nd and F streets. These are just a few brothels recalled by old-timers who were very young when prostitution and gambling flourished in Antioch And Pittsburg.

During Antioch's Chinatown era in 1882, several Chinese houses of prostitution were burned by the citizens and all the Chinese women inhabiting them were ran out of town. Only one woman, the wife of Yee Lee, was allowed to stay.

The fact that Antioch had a big vice problem was evidenced by a letter from Edwin E. Grant, law enforcement executive of the Contra Costa County District Attorney, to Antioch about flagrant violations of the Red Light Abatement. Part of his letter is reproduced..."To prevent any possibility of failure to locate the bawdy house in Antioch, I am sending you a diagram showing it's exact location. This diagram, however, should not be necessary since this particular bawdy house in Antioch has been known as one of the most notorious dens of vice in Contra Costa County and has been a stench in the nostrils of decent people in your county for many years. In fact, this building appears to have been built for the express purpose of a vice den." This was written in

1916. Finally in 1918, something was done about this particular bawdy house. It's name had changed to "Hazel's Place" but was still located on the corner of 3rd and K Streets. It was finally raided by the sheriff's office and three women were arrested. The Ledger said it took over a year to close the house and the raid had caused quite a bit of comment and the end of the affair was not over yet.

The Pittsburg Post and the Antioch Ledger was full of news about the red light districts, inhabitants and customers. Some of the items were...A cowboy fell of a red-light scow in Royce's Slough between Antioch and Pittsburg. He drowned. Another story was labeled, "Mysterious Drowning". It stated Clara Edwards, a woman of the underworld, occupying a house boat with 10 or 15 other women of her class in a slough between Pittsburg and Antioch was drowned in some manner not clear to the local officers. Another story was about a shooting. It related..." Man Shot on the Island... A man by the name of John McGraw with a bullet wound in his neck and otherwise somewhat disfigured in appearance, called Dr. Bauer at 6:00 AM for medical attention. He said he had been attacked by highwaymen. Later it was learned he had been involved in a shooting scrape sometime during the night at one of the dives on Coney Island (Winter's Island) across from Pittsburg."

Then on Oct. 7 1916 The Pittsburg Post had this sensational story with a big headline..."Red-light District Raided for Revenue Only. Biggest "Official" Holdup Ever Reported From Coney Island. "Gaiety" at Resorts Interrupted But Long Enough to Collect "Coin"...One of the biggest holdups ever reported from Coney Island was that of last Friday evening when Undersheriff Willie Veale, accompanied by three or four deputies, invaded the notorious red-light district for the obstensible purpose of closing the houses. The real purpose of the visit say the

168

women of the underworld, was that of collecting $100 apiece from the women in charge and $25 a head from the other inmates. One of the women is reported as saying this week that they are besieged from every official source for "protection" money; they have to pay all claims... some of which are none less surprising than would be a demand from the Governor of the State.

No one is of the opinion or belief that there is any intention on the part of the county officials to permanently close Cony Island. The "sensational" raid of last week was bunk pure and simple. An attempt was made to deceive the public. In coming to Coney Island the deputy sheriffs passed two or three ill-famed houses on the outskirts of Martinez. They evidently are in good standing with the officers...They are "protected" just as Coney Island is being protected...by the levying of tribute against those unfortunate women who are driven to every extremity of vice in order to meet the demands of the official vultures.

And let us say right here that there is not a shade difference between the officer who accepts the earnings of these women and the contemptible male being who relies on them for support.

Since the deputies were here last week Coney Island is said to be ablaze with red light and no uneasiness is felt by the women over the threatened closing of the resort. The only complaints heard are in the reference to the too frequent official holdups."

This story created a storm of controversy, on one side the officials said it wasn't true and Undersheriff W. M. Veale charged the editor, J. E. Tracy, with criminal libel in court. He retained all the star attorneys at the county seat to aid in the prosecution of the case. On the other hand, almost all the entire town of Pittsburg was behind the editor and they backed him almost 100%. The town raised his bail and prominent attorneys were

hired. Editorials from other newspapers also supported Editor Tracy's stand for the welfare of Pittsburg and general vicinity The Women's Improvement Club passed strong resolutions about Coney Island and they endorsed the editor's action and offered him moral support in any further action he might take in the matter.

Some of the headlines of the times was..."Hand of County Political Wing Shows Itself in Trumped-up Suit For Libel Against Editor of Post." and "Is an Attempt Being Made to Throttle the Press", also "Arresting of Inmates of Red-light Houses a Farce".

Finally on Nov. 18 1916, the criminal libel suit against J. F. Tracy, Editor of the Pittsburg Post, was settled out of court with Undersheriff William Veale. Both men claimed they misunderstood each other's statements. However, the Post said the houses should be closed if they are raided.

The Pittsburg Coney Island resorts (Winter's Island) were closed on Oct. 16 1916 by the Grand Jury under the Red Light Abatement Act. However, one of the owners of a resort reported that..... "Assurances had been given them that the places would be closed but for a few days." This must have been a true statement since in the Pittsburg Post of July 7, 1917 there were letters from the Governor and District Attorney to officers requesting them to close houses of prostitution in Contra Costa County. One of the complaints was that liquor was being sold to soldiers in uniform.

In 1917, the Grand Jury requested the County Supervisors to close the notorious road houses in Contra Costa County. It said these disreputable places in the western end of the county (Martinez, Pittsburg and Antioch) permitted gambling of all kinds, as well as other acts of lawlessness (prostitution), all of which was against the law and had been causing people to file complaints for months.

The Daily Ledger of Saturday, July 21, 1917 had a big story which is as follows..." Life Lost In "Ark"

Tragedy Last Monday. Was Clement Beirens Beaten Up Before Drowning ? Third in Life Toll Taken As The Result of Permitting Disreputable Red-light Scows On River... Two questions bothered the jury summoned by Deputy Coroner Fenton of Sacramento. Did Clement Beirens lose his life by being beaten-up in a general free-for-all fight and tossed overboard from the red-light houseboat lying in the river opposite Antioch, and conducted by Florence Hart, or did he accidentally fall in the river and drowned ?

The testimony given was flimsy at best. P. F. Blumberg, the speedboat man who ferried clients of the "arks" to and from Antioch's waterfront, said Beirens had asked him to take him back to Antioch and at that time the launch was alongside the scow dancehall. He said Beirens attempted to climb though the window of the scow and fell and knocked Blumberg into the river with him. Beirens sank to the bottom of the river and Blumberg said his shoulder was dislocated in the accident and he was unable to save the man. Ten witnesses were examined but little information was forthcoming. The women of the scows information consisted of the "I don't know" order. Florence Hart, owner of the red-light boat and scow, said all she heard was a splash and a call for help. She claimed there was no fight that night although there was trouble the night before.

Dr. W. S. George testified the man died from drowning but the condition of his head with cuts and bruises was suspected caused by other means. Others said the injuries were caused by brass knuckles. The jury found that Beirens came to his death by drowning but were not convinced it was an accident and recommended further investigation by the District Attorney of Sacramento. (the red-light scows were on the Sacramento County's side of the river and therefore in their jurisdiction) A second inquiry was made about the drowning but nothing new was brought out and the case was dropped.

As a result of this special inquiry it was bought to the attention of Sheriff Gormley of Sacramento that several "arks" were located at the west end of Sherman Island and should be ordered away. At first he declared there were no such places in his jurisdiction but after Antioch's Constable Whelihan and Justice of Peace James Taylor pointed out the exact location on the map, they went with him to the place and found six "arks" and two large dancehall scows with ten prostitutes aboard. They were told to leave the area. The Ledger said they moved a short distance west into Solano County and naturally will remain a pest to Antioch as ever.

In June 1918, the question of the red-light and gambling problems was raised at the meeting of the Antioch Town Trustees. Constable E. B. Whelihan asked for ordinances to close such places. He was told to forget about new ordinances and enforce ones already on the books. However, the trustees granted a renewal of John Arata's liquor license and a new one for Sam Black's place. The constable had been asked by well known persons to try to close the red-light houses and stop gambling, while others told him they should not be molested. There were editorials in the Daily Ledger about Antioch's problems with brothels and the ladies of the night. Among the complaints was the problem of the local decent women being accosted by men who thought they were prostitutes.

One mystery was solved with this story. Many ads in the old Pittsburg Post and Antioch Ledger newspapers of the era were for many speedboats and old photos show these sleek vessels. This was very puzzling as to how they managed to exist since there was plenty of river transportation to outlying towns. This story shows these boats were the principal transportation to and from the red-light "arks", scows and the islands of the bawdy houses.

Antioch in the year of 1996 doesn't seem to have a reputation for allowing prostitution to exist but Bay Point (West Pittsburg) still has a problem controlling the "ladies of the night". It seems that the world's "oldest profession" will continue to be with the area in one form or another.

FAST LAUNCH

Harry Herring now has one of the fastest speedboats on the river, having purchased a new craft in Stockton last week that is 28 feet long, has a 6-foot, 6-inch beam and is equipped with a Loew-Victor 40 horse-power engine that is capable of making from sixteen to seventeen miles an hour. He says the cabin is enclosed in such manner that the boat is comfortable in all kinds of weather and he can carry six or seven people in the cabin, or twelve to fourteen if necessary inside and on the deck together. He asks those who desire to make river trips to call and see him, as he also has another boat, which is open and suitable for summer trips.

Pictures of prostitutes from the 1907 Contra Costa Sheriff's Mug Book.
Courtesy of Contra Costa History Center

Scows and arks of the type that were used by prostitutes. From the San Fransisco Maritine Proctor Collection

RIVER SCENE, ANTIOCH, CALIF. 58/8

Some of the speed boats that carried passengers to the houses and arks of prostitution up and down the San Joaquin River. From Charles Bohakel Jr. Collection

174

House boats and houses on pilings at Antioch's water front where some "ladies of the night" plied their business. From Author's Collection

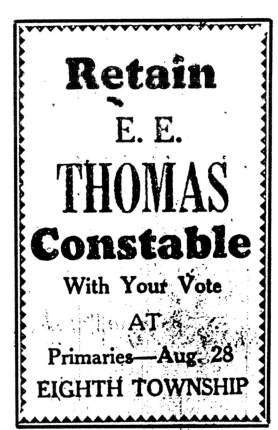

176

THE YACHT, "EL PRIMERO" REVISITED

In the first book "Looking Back", the story about the beautiful yacht "El Primero" was written in detail. This story was prompted by a mystery photograph of the yacht moored at the Antioch Lumber Company's dock. For at least 60 years and more, the story circulating about the picture was that the book-keeper of the lumber company owned the 110 foot vessel and lived aboard it. My comment was if he did, he had his hand deep in someone's pocket.

One day while visiting the present owner, Henry Beede whose family has been involved in the Antioch Lumber Company since 1871, I spied the original photo of the vessel on the wall of the old office and found the name of the yacht and the date it was built. From there it was a detective game finding the original owner and successive owners.

The National Maritime Museum, the California State Library and the old back issues of the Antioch Daily Ledger were the main instruments in solving the puzzle. A piece of information from one place would led to another bit of the story and finally it was complete. I found, during my research, the book-keeper, Frank Livingston, did own a boat, the 47 foot "Sapho", and lived aboard it.

The "El Primero", now over 100 years old, is still sailing as a charter boat in the waters of Vancouver, Canada. She is owned by Judy Kalke who has sent photos showing the yacht as it now appears at this time. After the first book was published, Thomas Youell, the grandson of Sidney A. "Sam" Perkins who was owner of the yacht for 44 years, contacted me and we exchanged photos of the vessel.

Perkins won the yacht in a poker or craps game in 1911. He was a famous newspaper publisher, steamship executive and banker. Perkins entertained four of country's presidents , Taft, Teddy Roosevelt, Harding, Hoover and other famous persons on the decks of "El Primero". President Taft was the one who gave him his nickname of "Sam". Perkins was probably the most influential publisher in the Pacific Northwest. He owned five newspapers. He was an executive of mining, investment and transportation firms and had the distinction of being friends of at least six Presidents of the United States.

His family were of moderate means and "Sam" Perkins as a boy found it necessary to work to earn money for his education. When he was a young man he borrowed 18,000 dollars to buy the Tacoma News and with that modest start built his newspaper and business empire. He was the one who said, "If Columbus had discovered the Pacific Coast, the Indians still would be trying to sell Manhatten Island for twenty-four dollars-----or less." Perkins was a devoted sailor and had the "El Primero" for 44 years until his death at 90 years of age.

During research for another article, I found photographs of the launching of the "El Primero" at the Bancroft Library of University of California, Berkley. These were shared with Tom Youell and Judy Kalke.

Youell sent blueprints of the yacht and many photos, including this one of his grandfather photographed on the deck of the yacht.

1893 Launching of "El Primero". From Bancroft Library Collection

Steam Yacht, "El Primero" 1893. From Bancroft Library Collection

"El Primero" ready to be Launched. From Bancroft Library Collection

August 5, 1893 Launching of Edwin Hopkins' dream yacht. From Bancroft Library Collection

"El Primero" on a cruise. From Tom Youell Collection

STEAM YACHT "EL PRIMERO"
S.A. PERKINS, TACOMA, U.S.A.

Steam yacht and Sidney "Sam" Perkins. From Tom Youell Collection

"Sam" Perkins with wife and the yacht. From Tom Youell Collection

"El Primero" blueprints by famous naval architect, Ed Gardner, commisioned by Tom Youell

"El Primero" at anchor. "Sam" Perkins, owner. From Tom Youell Collection

"El Primero" in 1895 winter dockage at Beede Lumber Yard, Antioch.
From Henry Beede Collection

The 1994 photographs of "EL Primero" Courtesy of owner, Judy Kalke

FERDINAND STAMM JR., BUILDER AND CITIZEN

The Stamm family is one of Antioch's oldest. Ferdinand Stamm Sr. was born in Hamburg, Germany and came to America in 1861 joining his brother, Louis. The young men came to San Fransisco but Ferdinand left to work the mines in Marysville. After that he worked in the manufacture of acids which was the type of work he did in Germany. He was offered a job in South San Fransisco in the distillery business and while occupied there he was offered a position with the Jost Distillery in Antioch.

Ferd Sr. took the job and moved to Antioch in 1871. His brother, Louis, followed him and established a shoe store on G street. In 1873, Ferdinand married Marie Jost of the distillery family and Ferdinand Jr. was born in 1875. By 1898, The Stamm Family owned a very large property located from A Street to the riverfront on which the father had established a vineyard and produced wine.

Ferdinand Stamm Jr. attended the local schools and went to work at the Antioch Lumber Company about 1890. A newspaper article in 1898 had a story about the installation of an 8 ton cooker at the Distillery that was being done by three persons. Twenty three year old Ferd Jr. was one of them. The three men had to raise the cooker 20 feet without the use of modern equipment and had to rely wholly on skill and steady nerves while raising the 8 ton vessel using timbers and a screw device. It was installed in less than a week and young Stamm had found his vocation.

He formed a partnership in the building business with Barney Riley. Highly successful in that business, his interest expanded and he went into the general contracting business with Fred Peters. When Mr. Peters left Antioch, Ferd assumed full charge of the business.

When his father died in 1911, Ferdinand Stamm Jr. was always referred to as Ferd Stamm. Before the turn of the century, he married Ethel Dahnken whose family was a member of the famous Turner and Dahnken Theater organization. Her family was also old time Antioch residents. A son, George, and a daughter, Lolita, was born to the parents, Ferd and Ethel.

Ferd Stamm entered the business of entertainment for the public in 1906 by operating the old Pavilion as a skating rink in partnership with Fred Peters and Roy Beede. The Pavilion was located in what is known today as the Casino building on Waldie Plaza.

The first movie house in Antioch was Turner and Dahnken's Majestic located at 639 2nd Street. They quit showing the one reel movies and rented them to Stamm who with a new partner, Dr. D. E. Hawley, opened a new skating rink back of the Antioch Hotel in 1907. Two or three movie shows were screened each week at the rink which was at 1st And G Streets. Four years later, the competition from the new Belshaw Building with it's better stage and dance floor caused Stamm to consider remodeling the Pavilion into an up-to-date movie theater.

Ferd and Ralph Beede joined to do the project with Ferd and his workmen doing the remodeling of the brick building. The roof was raised three feet and the floor lowered to make a sloping floor for the seats. A stage was built at the north end of the building with dressing rooms underneath the stage. While excavating the new basement, an Indian burial ground was discovered. A twenty foot extension was added to the south end to provide a foyer, ticket office and projection room. The new theater opened on Saturday, Oct. 7, 1911 as the Casino Theater offering movies and high class vaudeville acts. It was considered the handsomest and best equipped moving picture house in the county. It served the town for seventeen years until Ferd and Ralph built the pretentious El Campanil Theater.

In most of the issues of the Ledger there are stories of Ferd Stamm or his company. The toughest of jobs were undertaken and accomplished with sheer business ability, in straight thinking and in a common sense approach to the problems. Ferd built most of Antioch's larger buildings, among them was the Safeway on G Street and the huge Hickmott Cannery warehouse. He built and moved buildings all over the county. He and his crew were specialists in moving brick buildings. His crowning triumph was his "El Campanil Theater" and it still stands today in all it's splendor. Among many of his completed tasks was moving the Methodist Church from G Street to 6th Street and moving the big Antioch Hotel from 2nd Street to 1st Street. These were just a few of the many undertakings that Ferd accomplished with verve.

Stamm was an outstanding example of a self-made man. Starting literally with nothing at the time of his marriage, he became, in a short period of time, one of the most outstanding figures of Antioch and one of the wealthiest

Ferd Stamm took pride in his home town and worked diligently without pay to improve the growth of Antioch from a town into a city. His community service was a record of thirty five years starting with Ferd joining the Volunteer Antioch Fire Company in 1902. At that time it consisted of one hose cart and one ancient pumper, all hand pulled to the fires. In 1906, he became the Fire Chief and held that position until his death in 1937.

He was one of the town's trustees (councilman) from 1910 until 1916. While in that position, he saw that the Fire Department got the new equipment it needed. That included the first mechanical truck, the 1916 Ford Fire Engine. In 1928, he returned to the Antioch Council for another nine years service during which time he was also the Police Commissioner. While on the council, he pushed for Antioch's new high pressure water system that resulted in lower fire insurance for the town.

Ferd played football and baseball as a young man. He was a big, husky, handsome youngster and one in demand when it came to sports. He played on the Antioch town baseball team in 1910. He played a big part in the Fire Hose Cart races in competition with other towns.

Ferd Stamm was a generous man, although his gifts were seldom publicized. He helped groups such as the boy scouts and his generosity toward friends was a byword. He put down the grass turf that covered the playing field of the Municipal Stadium. Ferd aided Antioch's famous American Legion Football Team with money and support.

In 1935, his son, George Stamm, was admitted to full partnership after working with his father for several years and the firm's name of "F. Stamm & Son" was adopted. The fact that Ferd was one of Contra Costa County's wealthiest citizens brought no vanity or false pride to him. He and his family lived in a conservative house on quiet B Street and there was no affectation of dress or manner in Ferd's life. No stranger would have recognized him as other than an ordinary resident.

A great tribute to Ferdinand Stamm Jr., at the time of his death in 1937, was the closing of all Antioch businesses and all flags were flown at half--mast during his funeral services. Only one other citizen was accorded that honor and that was Henry Fuller Beede.

Ferdinand Stamm Jr. 1875-1937   Courtesy of Stamm Family

Two of Ferd Stamm's fleet of big trucks. These are hauling straw for the paper mill.
Courtesy of Stamm Family

Ralph Beede, Stamm's partner in theaters.
Courtesy of Henry Beede

YOUTHS REPRIMANDED

Patrons of the Casino Theatre gave John Hadley generous applause Wednesday night, following a severe reprimand delivered to three local youths who were annoying the audience by bursting paper bags and making unnecessary noise. These lads have been making a practice of whistling, talking and screeching at every opportunity, until many complaints were made against their conduct. Patience ceasing to be a virtue, Hadley gave them a good lecture, telling them they were welcome to attend the performance if they behaved, but if not to remain away. Not a sound was heard during his talk, but that his remarks were appropriate and appreciated was shown by the hand-clapping.

ADDED TO LIBRARY FUND

A few more dollars were added to the treasury of the library Tuesday evening, from the entertainment in the Casino Theatre. However, the attendance was not what it should have been, owing to the disagreeable night. The film, "The Girl of the Lost Lake," was very good and in addition Mrs. Nellie Beede Kelley rendered two very excellent vocal solos in her usual gracious manner. It is the intention to give other similar entertainments during the coming spring months, announcement of which will be made later.

THE EL CAMPANIL THEATER

Ferd Stamm and Ralph Beede saw the theatrical and movie house business grow steadily in size starting from the early 1900s. They saw it grow from a one reel motion picture house to the culmination of the magnificent "El Campanil" Theater. The two men started their partnership in 1911 when they built the Casino Theater by converting the old Pavilion skating rink into a modern (by 1911 standards) movie and vaudeville theater. The Casino Building is located on the northeast corner of Waldie Plaza. The partners' theater served the community for seventeen years during which time the one reeler became obsolete and was replaced by ten and twelve reel pictures. The vaudeville stage and movie theater was outgrown as the population of Antioch increased.

Ralph and Ferd decided it was time to build a new theater and made their move in 1927. Starting Oct. 30, 1927, Ferd Stamm wrecked the building occupied by the William Wren Insurance Agency at the northwest corner of 2nd and G Streets. On Wednesday, Nov. 2nd, a large Stamm crew started work on the Antioch Hotel which was moved to the rear of the property facing 1st Street. The new theater was estimated to cost $500,000.00 and was planned to be completed in 6 to 7 months. The property, 75 by 200 feet, had been owned by the partners for the previous three years and bought for the purpose of building the new theater. The excavation for the building started as soon as the Antioch Hotel was on it's foundation. Stamm had determined the foundation specifications before the detailed plans for the theater were completed by the architects.

The plans finally arrived and the front elevation was displayed in the front window of the Nozilia Market, creating great excitement for the community. The building is of the Mission style of architecture with three belfries. The center belfry was occupied by the old Grammar School bell. When the workmen installed it

they had great fun making it ring with gusto. The name picked for the new theater was "El Campanil" which was selected for it's meaning in Spanish, "The Bell Towers".

The theater, overbuilt for lasting permanence, is constructed of reinforced concrete and steel. The "El Campanil" was beautiful to see inside and out. The exterior was painted light tan with the ornamentation in light gray, the belfry niche panels were Venetian red with black grill work. The windows of the upstairs offices were trimmed in black.

The marquee was a warm gray trimmed in yellow, green and gold. The ticket office was brass and black tile, the lobby was done in ivory with green and black mosaic stenciling. The inner lobby had a ceiling of orange while the walls were green, highlighted in gold. The foyer was a sight to see in richness and beauty. The large restrooms are located off the foyer. Directly in the front was the drinking fountain with full length mirrors on either side. The four interior wall panels showed the Moorish influence; red, black, blue and yellow over a background of gold and silver, all the rest was ivory and gold. Four arches divided the ceiling into five panels, the subdued colors of the arches contrasted with gold. The arches were banded with thick twisted gold rope. The walls facing the lobby were cream and gold.

The interior of the theater was of Spanish Renaissance period influenced by Moorish. The ceiling was soft orange, the walls of red and gold tapestry. Three niches on each side wall were blue, yellow, gold, silver and green. The grills were black and the posts on each side of the niches were dark blue, the pilasters were silver, gray and blue; trimmed in red and green. The organ lofts were decorated in the same colors as the side niches.

There were eight pendant ceiling lamps of Moorish design and two nude female statues placed above the center of the huge arch that frames the stage. If you think the colors are garish by today's standards, it wasn't in 1928. In fact, the interior decoration was done by William Chevalas, a famous theater interior designer.

The seats were upholstered, the loge seats were luxurious furniture type and an audience of 1200 could be seated in the theater. A $15,000.00 organ was installed, also the stage had a piano. The dressing rooms were in the basement. The theater lighting system was equipped with a three color light system, red, blue and amber. In each of the eight ceiling lights there were 12 lamps of each color, making a total of 36 lamps in each unit. The stage lighting also used those colors in the footlights and overhead lights. The three color system was used in combination to provide mood changes in the audience. The projection room was a model of efficiency

The "El Campanil Theater" was featured in "Motion Picture News" in 1928. The magazine devoted two pages in the article about Stamm and Beede's new theater. The second time the magazine ever gave a new theater that much space in their publication.

The theater's grand opening was Nov. 1, 1928, one year after the start of construction. It was one opening that had the county talking. Ralph Beede made a special trip to San Francisco to get an outstanding film. Every seat was sold and theater parties planned for the event.

However, the big parade on Oct. 31 was the ultimate in ballyhoo! The huge "Theater Opening Announcement Caravan" started at 1 o'clock and it was the largest and most enthusiastic auto parade that has ever traveled the county highways. With three traffic officers (including the County Highway Patrol) mounted on motorcycles to clear the way, led by Mayor James Donlon and city officials, the long caravan went out the highway to Oakley and Brentwood. Circling back, it passed through Antioch with noisy acclaim,

on through Pittsburg, Bay Point to Martinez and back though Clyde and Concord. There were 80 autos decorated with banners in the parade and 38 of them were sponsored by Antioch's civic organizations and businesses. That caravan certainly did tell the county with honking horns, sirens and shouts that the "El Campanil Theater" would be open the next day.

The opening program on Nov. 1st included a vaudeville program with 11 persons and the special movie was "Moran of the Marines" featuring Richard Dix and Ruth Elder, big stars in 1928.

By April 9, 1929, the "El Campanil" had sound equipment and a special screen installed for the new talking pictures at the cost of $25,000.00.

Many stars appeared on the stage of the "El Cmpanil" including Roy Rogers, Donald O'Conner, Smiley Burnette (movie teammate of Gene Autrey), Edgar Bergen and his wooden pal, Charlie McCarthy, Sally Rand and her fan (she penned a poem on one of the wall vents in the basement) and many other movie stars made their appearances on the theater's vaudeville programs. The big bands played to enthusiastic crowds and among them were Jimmy Dorsey, Tommy Dorsey, Paul Whiteman, Louie Armstrong and Red Nickels and his Five Pennies.

Several years after the theater opened, Ferd Stamm bought out his partner, Ralph Beede and his son, George Stamm, became a partner with his father. Today, George Stamm Jr. is the president of the organization his grandfather and father founded.

Drawing of El Campanil Theater by famous theater designer, William Chavalas

EL CAMPANIL THEATRE

ANTIOCH, CALIFORNIA

Stamm & Beede, Proprietors

GRAND OPENING THURSDAY EVE., NOVEMBER 1, 1928		SPECIAL PROGRAM VAUDEVILLE ACTS MOTION PICTURES

THE BEST IN ENTERTAINMENT FOR DIABLO VALLEY AT ALL TIMES

Enterprise of Pride and Confidence

 EL CAMPANIL THEATER presents to the public one of the greatest single assets of Antioch and Diablo Valley. By far the most pretentious building in all of Contra Costa County and perhaps not having a peer in Central California, it is a monument to its builders and owners, a pride to the community it serves, and a distinguishing feature in a city which holds a future fully justifying the enterprise which has been shown.

El Campanil, the tower of bells, is Spanish in design as well as name, exemplifying the spirit of pioneers of California who showed their faith in the land to which they had come in search of fortunes, and to spend their lives. So El Campanil but repeats history— it exemplifies the spirit of confidence possessed by its owners in the city of which they are native sons, where they have hopes to prosper and firmly believe that Antioch holds today every advantage for a continued development and a place of importance.

They are optimistic but justly so. They, native sons of Antioch, are but exhibiting the confidence which strengthened the pioneers to face

RALPH M. BEEDE

Photo taken especially for The Antioch Ledger by the Smith Studio.

the work before them. El Campanil stands today the full embodiment of their faith.

The undertaking is the biggest private undertaking of the community, the possession of two individuals, displaying enterprise of a high standing.

Ferdinand Stamm and Ralph Beede are the sons of Antioch pioneers. They have been associated in the theatrical business in Antioch since 1911, when they became owners of the present Casino Theater, in its day one of the best show houses, but now relegated to the discard to give way to modern and beautiful El Campanil. They have seen the motion picture business grow from an infant undertaking to the

FERD STAMM

Photo taken especially for The Antioch Ledger by the Smith Studio.

principal entertainment of the public. They have seen it change from simple entertainment to that of the highest order, they have seen the introduction of educational features, the showing of pictures to stir the emotions of multitudes, the creation of entertainment for all ages, all classes.

Mr. Stamm, devoting his principal energies to the building business, has been the contractor in charge of the construction of El Campanil. It is a permanent exhibit of his ideal —to build beautifully. Nothing more need be said of him. He is known too well throughout the county, and a visit to El Campanil will show more than thousands of words could tell.

His son, George, is his general assistant and plays an important part in the execution of the contracting and building business.

Mr. Beede, manager of the Antioch Lumber Company, is likewise without need of introduction. He has also acted as business manager for the theatrical enterprise of the partnership. To him is due the credit of selecting the furnishings for the accommodation of El Campanil's patrons, and all will agree that he, too, has demonstrated a full understanding of his business.

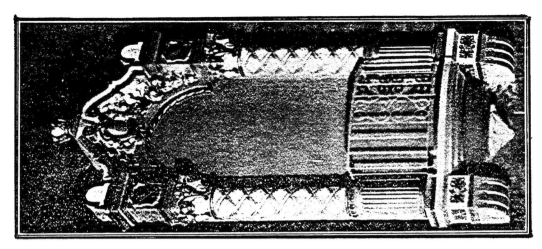

One of 6 wall niches.

Seating arrangement and stage of El Campanil Theater.

One of the grilles for the Wurlitzer pipe organ loud speakers.

Lobby of the El Campanil Theater.

Theater is almost completed 1928.

El Campanil Usherettes from the 1940 era. From Stamm Collection

El Campanil Theater House Orchestra, 1940 era. From Stamm Collection

Antioch's El Campanil Theater in the 1940's. From Stamm Collection

River life may have looked serene and comfortable in the early days of Antioch, Pittsburg and other places on the river front, but it was really a dangerous way of life for many.

Many mishaps befell unthinking rivermen, especially those whom spent too much time imbibing in one of the many riverside saloons of the river towns and Antioich and Pittsburg had their share of saloons. Fog also caused boat accidents, as did greed and plain stupidity. Luck also played a large part in how the toss of destiny dice landed. Many were saved but many were not.

River trade was vital, in that era, to the welfare of towns such as Antioch and Pittsburg because there were no roads nor railroads and all goods, travelers and mail arrived by boat. The news of the vessels was a prime concern to the citizens of these communities, and the Antioch Ledger and Pittsburg-Post Dispatch constantly carried news of the comings and goings of the vessels. What happened on the Sacramento and San Joaquin Rivers made front page news from 1870 to 1928.

Antioch was the last deep-water port on the San Joaquin River and much of the grain, animals, vegetables, hay, coal, canned goods, fish and other products were shipped by deep--water sailing vessels and steamers to U. S. ports and around the world. Low-draft steamers and other riverboats made their way to Stockton and Sacramento stopping at river and slough landings to pick up and drop off passengers, produce, supplies and mail. The rivers and their tributaries were the highways of the time and accidents were bound to happen.

Stories of river happenings taken from the Daily Ledger and Post Dispatch show how important river travel was during those times. Besides shipping and receiving goods and the carrying of passengers, there were excursions. For example, the Lauritzen Brother's boat, "The Emperess", made trips to San Fransisco in the early 1900s.

The Lauritzens sailed their vessel, carrying 80 passengers, to view the U. S. Navy battleship fleet that was visiting San Fransisco at that time.

Local companies also hosted pleasure trips by steamer, while baseball fans took excursions to other river towns where local teams were playing. The "Caroline", the oldest riverboat running from San Fransisco to Stockon, hosted many excursions in the early 1900s.

Fires caused many casualties in the early days. A fire in 1870 badly damaged a sloop anchored across the river from Antioch. It caught fire caused by sparks from the galley smokestack. Captain Turner and the steamer, "Antioch", went to her assistance and tried to get her captain to scuttle the vessel in order to put out the flames where vessel was anchored. The sloop's captain wanted to be closer to Antioch and Turner towed and sank the vessel offshore of the distillery (near the Antioch Lumberyard) but the sloop was badly damaged by then

The 50 foot "Princess" of the Lauritzen Transportation Co. was mysteriously burned at Lauritzen's wharf at the foot of I Street in Antioch at about 1:30 AM on Dec. 28, 1915. The fire also destroyed a shed, but firefighters saved the office building.

In 1916, the personal launch of George "The Potato King" Shima was destroyed by fire when the engine backfired and ignited the gasoline tank. The story in the Antioch Ledger reported that it was the most luxurious launch on the river and cost $4000.

The towboat "Diablo" was burned and sank one mile east of the Antioch Bridge in 1928. The engine backfired and the resulting fire got out of control. The men aboard jumped onto the towed barge and cut it loose, saving their lives.

Three died when the riverboat "Stanley Robert" struck a load of pipe underwater near Pittsburg, overturned and sank. A barge loaded with pipe was being towed by the tug "Panama" when it collided with the motor vessel

"Sonoma". The pipe fell overboard where it became a hidden menace, causing the accident of the "Stanley Robert" the next day because there were no markers at the site. The vessel was towed to Antioch's Fulton Shipyard were she had been originally built and they repaired her at cost of $20,-000. The vessel was renamed "Swastika".

In 1889, within a radius of ten miles of Antioch and Pittsburg, 120 boats employed 350 salmon and sturgeon fishermen. They fished nine months of the year and the average daily catch was 3,000 fish. The fish was packed in ice and shipped to the eastern market. Most of the fisherman were Greek and Italians. These men and their boats had their share of accidents on the water. On June 9, 1898, the fishing boat of George Balabacas and John Morisos capsized on the flats of Suisun Bay near Grizzly Island during a heavy gale and both men were drowned.

Another Ledger story told of an Italian fisherman who left Three-Mile Slough for Antioch in his fishing smack. The sail was too large for the boat and the fisherman experienced considerable trouble tacking the boat down the San Joaquin River, because the boat's bow was continually shooting up in the air while the stern was skirting the under-edge of the white-capped waves. Finally the boat turned completely over and the occupant was thrown into the river, but later scrambled onto the bottom of his over--turned boat. Sandy Lambro, Antioch's legendary Greek fisherman, was rowing up the river in his skiff and he rescued the man. They tied ropes to the over-turned boat and rowed to shore. It took them all afternoon to tow the boat and make a landing.

Many of the sailors and passengers in those early river days fell overboard and never came up again. Many local children drowned swimming and playing on the river. Other drowning victims were captains and sailors who had too much to drink at the local saloons and lost their footing trying to board their vessels at night.

The many Chinese who plied the river in their sampans also were involved in collisions with steamers, sailing vessels and had other types of accidents in the late 1800s.

Boilers explosions and collisions of large vessels happened very often and these accidents were usually disastrous. Boilers used by the steam engines to propel steamers were not always reliable and many exploded from unwise use or bad repair.

In July 1871, the Antioch Ledger reported on a fatal accident on the steam paddle-wheel boat called the "Antioch". The vessel was built in 1885 (Probably at the Jarvis Shipyard since it was the only yard in Antioch at that time. That shipyard later became the Fulton Shipyard.). The "Antioch" was a 70 ton paddle-wheel steamer, powered by a 25 horsepower engine, which ran a regular ferry service between Collinsville and Antioch. While stopping at Brown's Landing on the lower end of Sherman Island, the steam drum exploded. Two men standing in the pilot-house, V. Blanchard and a Chinese man, were fatally scalded by the steam that filled the house.

An investigation found the owner, Abraham Turner, had the boiler repaired by "corking" it at the New York Landing (Pittsburg). Engineers examining the damaged boiler said it was unsafe before the accident. Capt. Turner and his two brothers insisted they knew nothing about the unsafe condition or the "corking" of the boiler. However the vessel's fireman testified the boiler had been "corked" at New York Landing six week prior to the explosion.

The coroner's report..."The death of V. Blanchard (nothing was mentioned about the dead Chinese man) was caused by the explosion of the steam drum, which was unsafe to use at the time. The boat owners knew of this, and it was through their negligence that the accident happened." Capt. Turner nevertheless did not lose his license as a result of the accident.

202

One of the most terrible river disasters in California happened aboard the steamer, "T. C. Walker" at 4:30 a.m. on a Sunday in late November 1889. Just after the boat left Turner's Landing and while in the vicinity of Fourteen-Mile Slough, the steam drum exploded and seven persons were killed and six injured. Cause of the accident was never determined. All the victims were killed by the concussion or scalded to death by the escaping steam. The captain, chief engineer and his wife, and one of the firemen were among the victims. The Antioch Ledger said the new steamer "H. J. Corcoran" would be put on the run until the "T C. Walker" could be repaired, at a cost of $4000.

The California Navigation and Improvement Company, owner of these vessels had more than it's share of bad luck that year. It started with the sinking of the "Leader" by the "J.D.Peters". The "Leader" was on it's way from Stockton with a band of sheep on the lower-deck and about 100 patients from the Stockton asylum in the upper-- deck staterooms enroute to Napa. Signals were misread and the "Leader" was cut down and sunk. The sheep were drowned but all the passengers were saved.

Later, a lamp exploded on the "Mary Garratt" and all her upper works were destroyed before the fire was extinguished Then came the sinking of the "J. D. Peters". She was on her regular trip between Stockton and San Fransisco with a load of Chinese passengers when there was a collision with the vessel, "Czarina", on the San Fransisco Bay, and she sank. A reward of $20 was offered by one of the Chinese Companies of San Fransisco for the bodies of any of the Chinese who were drowned.

The fast new steamer "H. J. Corcoran" was built in the summer of 1898 in the shipyards of the California Navigational and Improvement Co. of Stockton. The paddle-wheel steamer was powered by two high pressure boilers. Her interior was painted with four or more coats of white paint, the pursuer's office was of polished wood. There was a smoking room around the smokestack forward. All the staterooms opened out to the deck and also on the inside into the main cabin. the beds were of the latest wire-spring variety and each room was furnished with a patent wash basin and lighted by electricity.

On the way to Antioch and Pittsburg, one of the vessel's first trial trips, her paddle-wheel...owing to a miscalculation of her builders...was set too deep in the water and caught in the mud. She was towed back to Stockton. On her official trial trip, she failed to make San Fransisco because of machinery problems. She was laid up for several weeks at the Stockton shipyard. By Sept. 10, 1898, the "H. C. Corcoran" was making her regular runs, however, on one of them she ran into Antioch's steamboat wharf. The damage was heavy as she ripped up the planks on the wharf and twisted and broke heavy timbers.

Not all accidents on the river had disastrous effects. The steamer "Navaho" enroute from Sacramento to San Fransisco, ran aground near West Pittsburg (now Bay Point) in 1913. The ferryboat "Bridget" of the Oakland, Antioch and Eastern Railroad came to the rescue and transferred 100 passengers to the wharf at Pittsburg. The passengers completed their journey to San Fransisco on the O.A.&E.'s electric railroad.

Other accidents also had happy endings. In 1913 at Antioch, Father F. Lawernce was on the city wharf waiting for the up-river boat, when he heard someone calling for help and found a man clinging to a piling. When the rescuers tried to pull him up, he refused until they accepted an old violin first. As the musician was standing on the wharf, shivering from his impromptu bath, he was asked where he came from. He answered and said... "I don't know, but I was on my way somewhere when I fell in." That was all that could be learned from him.

Salvadore Bruno of Pittsburg was saved from drowning by his dog, Buster. When Bruno fell off his boat near the Antioch Bridge, crippling an arm when it happened, his dog, a large Airdale, jumped in the river and swam to his master. Bruno grasped the dog by the scruff of the neck with his uninjured hand and urged the dog to swim back to the boat. The craft was low-decked and Bruno managed to pull himself aboard and helped the tired canine out of the water.

Lauritzen Transportation Company's "Ellen" and "Princess"
at Antioch I Street dock. From the Lauritzen Collection

Lauritzen's "Empress" on the Sacramento River
From the Lauritzen Collection

The river boat "Sutter" built at Antioch's Fulton Shipyard. Now used as the San Joaquin Yacht Club building. From the Fulton Shipyard Collection

Steamboat race in the 1930s. "Pride of the River", "Cherokee" and third boat unknown. From the Charles Bohakel Jr. Collection

Three river boats loaded with sacks of vegetables.
From the Charles Bohakel Jr. Collection

The "Marin", riverboat owned by Fay and Son based at Rio Vista.
Built by Fulton Shipyard. From the Fulton Shipyard Collection

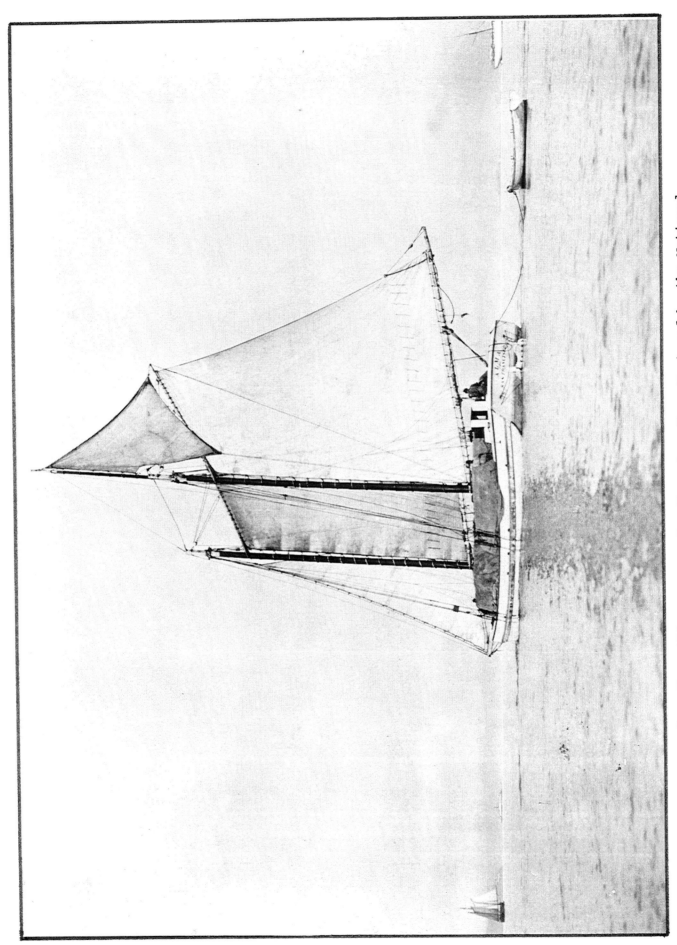

The "Alma", sailing scow on San Fransisco Bay. Restored by the National
Maritine Museum in San fransisco. From the National Maritime Collection

The "Fort Bragg" loading potatoes at Potato Slough. From the Charles Bohakel Jr. Collection

The "Delta Queen" on the Sacramento River. From Charles Bohakel Jr. Collection

"H. J. Corcoran" New fast steamer , built 1898 by the California Navigation and Improvement Co. Courtesy of Contra Costa History Center

Sailing vessel and river sailing scow with load of hay. From Charles Bohakel Jr. Collection

Two Pittsburg salmon fishermen sailing to the fishing grounds. From Charles Bohakel Jr. Collection

Typical early riverboat on the San Joaquin or Sacramento River.
From the Charles Bohakel Jr. Collection

The "Delta King" and passengers. Now used as a resturant and hotel in Sacramento. From the Charles Bohakel Jr. Collection

The "Utility", gasoline powered river barge owned by the Antioch Lumber Company. From the Henry Beede Collection

The Riverview Union High School District was formed in 1903 when Henry F. Beede organized a movement to bring four elementary districts together to form a high school district. These districts were Antioch, Black Diamond (Pittsburg), Somersville and Carbondale. Live Oak district joined the union later. An election on June 1903 approved of the high school district.

Antioch was selected as the site for the new high school because Antioch had the most students and was more centrally located in the new district.

In 1909, The California State Legislature passed a bill or law authorizing union high school districts that had been in existence for three years to build a school building. The bill allowed the districts to levy a one year tax to pay for the building.

The high school district bought 2.5 acres of property on A Street near the city park in 1908. The trustees planned to build the new building there but a bond election for that purpose of $20,000 was defeated. The Pittsburg residents were the cause of the defeat. They wanted a high school building in their town and they were opposed to the Antioch site.

In 1909, C. A. Hooper, the owner and developer of property in Antioch and Pittsburg (including all the property between the two towns), offered to give land for the new high school building. In 1910, the trustees accepted C. A. Hooper's donation of two blocks of land west of the Fibreboard Paper Mill on the road between Antioch and Black Diamond (Pittsburg).

The trustees budgeted the cost of the school building at $17,000.00. In the summer of 1910, the well-known firm of architects, Cumming & Weymouth of Oakland were awarded the contract for furnishing the plans and specifications for the building. They submitted three exterior plans and one interior plan.

Sketches of three different styles of structures were made by the architects. The first, and thought by some critics as the most modern and beautiful of all, showed a very artistic mission style building, being brick covered with cream colored plaster, the window casings, door casings and roof being red color. The second gave a square effect with a comparatively small amount of ornamental work, the walls being faced with buff brick and the building having a low appearance on account of a low roof. The third design was not considered to be modern in looks as the other two, the walls showing red brick, heavy ornamental caps over both windows and doors and provided with a high roof. The conservative trustees selected the third design and the interior plans were entirely satisfactory and approved by the trustees. The interior had ten large rooms on the main floor with each room opening on a wide corridor running the entire length of the building. These rooms were occupied by the language class, commercial recitation and drawing class, library, science and mathematics, English recitation class, history recitation and typewriting rooms. The study hall was the largest being 30x40 feet and provided with a large stage. The principal's office and the teacher's room was also on the main floor.

In the basement, which is really the ground floor, was the domestic and science laboratory rooms, the boys and girls lunch rooms (each had a separate room), chemical and physics room and the manual training room. Also the furnace room.

It was the most complete school building in the county and being located on the high ground overlooking the river lived up to it's name of Riverview Union High School.

Construction of the new high school was started in September of 1910. It was hoped to be completed in a few months but that did not happen. While the building was being constructed, representatives from other school districts visited the site expressing their desire for a similar structure to be built in their district. The school building was finally completed and the formal dedication and opening took place on November 11, 1911. Students arrived at the school on the railroad, river boat and bus during the school season.

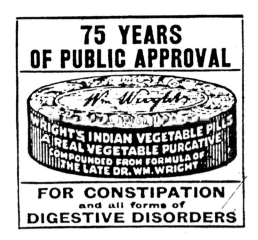

Riverview Union High School. Built 1911. From Author's Collection

Riverview Union Manual Training Building. Constructed 1916 by students.
From Author's Collection

Riverview Union High School Track Team, 1916 . Notice framing of
the Manual Arts Building in Background. From Author's Collection

Riverview Union Football Team, 1916. More framing up on Manual Arts Building.
From Author's Collection

When the Riverside Union High School needed a manual training building and the funds were limited, the school trustees and the manual training instructor had the answer. Let the students build the building and get the practical experience that books couldn't give them. The high school, located in Antioch, became one of the very few schools in the State of California, if not the only one, to accomplish the building of a structure of this size. The goal was a building that met the specifications, would be a creditable structure and the teaching of construction methods to the unskilled students who comprised the working force.

One of the first problems was the location of the foundation. The boys were asked to find the proper place, having one corner stake given. Many of the young workmen learned that a building was not placed just anywhere like a straw stack in a forty acre field. They did considerable thinking before the final stakes were set and the location proved by a transit. They then started the excavation for the cement foundation. When that was finished the boys filled it with cement that they mixed.

The boys having not the slightest idea of construction work were taught by George H. Cater, the manual training instructor. He had to explain more fully than if he had been working with hired labor. The weather was hot and unpleasant but the boys went at it with a will and showed by their interest that doing things appealed to them. Also they did not have to stay indoors studying while working on the building.

The finished building was a remarkable substantial structure. The construction was heavier than was normal in other buildings on the west coast of California. The floor timbers were placed on a solid concrete foundation instead of piers. The floor joists, studding and other framing materials were chosen above the margin of safety. The building had many windows and was a two story structure

It was built in sections which allowed the using of more boys to advantage since all of them were not fitted for some of the work. While it was the aim of the instructor to employ every boy, at times there were tasks that only certain boys could accomplish. Physical fitness had to be considered as well as personal traits and skills.

The building was sheathed and then weather boarded with rustic resawn lumber and finished with batten exterior casing. This type of construction required a great amount of fitting and while it was not always as good as journeymen carpenter's work it stood up against houses erected with similar materials. No claim was made that the building was perfect but from a practical viewpoint this was a shop structure and not an ornamental house. From all around consideration, conception, lines, accuracy, appearance and utility it was admitted the structure was a success and the young builders were highly commended for their zeal.

One third of the building was planned for the shop area and the rest for teaching purposes. While the building was being constructed, the scaffolding was a special problem since it often had to carry more than the normal load of workmen. Since these workmen were boys gifted with all the heedlessness of boys whose mothers at home, who, no doubt had misgivings as to their children working in the heights. Fortunately there were no mishaps during the construction of the building and the manual training instructor said the only injury was an occasional hammered thumb.

The time expended to construct the building took almost a year to finish it. Although it was a time consuming project, the boys thought it was fun. For them it was a far better way to enjoy school then to spend time in a stuffy class room.

The thought behind the boys building their shop building was to improve their minds and give them practical experience to find jobs after graduation of their class. Today, it would seem more of this type of education should be used for modern boys and girls to prepare them to compete in the real competition for jobs.

The Manual Arts Building was back of the brick school building that is now the Riverview Fire District's office. It was located in the northwest corner of the District's rear parking lot.

The Riverview school building was in use until 1931. A new high school building was constructed in Antioch on D Street and the old school was closed. Several different firms leased or bought the building during the period of 1931 until 1995. One firm was the Louisiana-Pacific Company who used the building as their laboratory. They, in turn, leased the building to the Riverview Fire District in 1975. The building is now owned by the Fire District.

MANUAL TRAINING

With the coming of Mr. Cater a new system has been introduced into this department. Instead of merely making small desks, chairs, and other articles of furniture, the boys have built two buildings. The first was a small shed for the janitor and the second a large manual training building. This is a very attractive, being low, two stories in height, stained brown. The boys have done all the work on it.

Riverview Union High School Baseball Team, 1916. From Author's Collection

The Johnson and Lanteri Shipyard was located on the south bank of New York Slough about 3/4 of a mile east of Pittsburg. It is now the site of the USS-POSCO steel mill. The shipyard built all types of vessels including ferry boats, dredgers, tow boats and barges. They were also marine designers and some of the best gasoline tow-boats ever built in the Bay area was their design. The yard was particularly well located, having a deep water port so sea-going vessels could unload lumber and materiel on their wharf. Southern Pacific and Santa Fe Railroads had spur tracks leading into their property. It was near the Delta country where all the dredgers were operating.

The shipyard operated from 1909 until 1921 and during that time built some of the largest dredgers in the world. The first dredges built by Johnson and Lanteri were " Monterey" and "Tule King" in 1910. The "Tule King" was captained by Land Maupin who with Lanteri built, in 1911, the second aeroplane, and a highly successful one, ever constructed in California.

As many as 90 to 170 men were employed at the shipyard and the monthly payroll was approximately $4000 and this was good wages in that time.

They built 68 big pontoons that were used by the government dredgers, "Sacramento" and "San Joaquin", in laying the pipelines. They also built those two dredgers in 1913. The vessels were 350 ton dredgers and 170 men were employed building them. The two vessels were used to lay the oil and gasoline pipe lines upriver.

The Pittsburg Post mentions repairs made on the Lauritzens' launches, "Duchess" and "Ellen", at Johnson and Lanteri Shipyard. This is quite surprising as the Lauritzens owned their own shipyard in Antioch. It would be interesting to know what caused having those vessels repaired at the J & L Yard.

J. A. Johnson, an experienced dred- ger builder and designer, and B. P. Lanteri, who was an expert ship designer and shipwright, gave their dredgers the first steel sides and large wooden arches as hull stiffeners. Both men were imaginative and able designers.

Lanteri and Johnson, in 1914, built two of the largest dredgers ever const- ructed in the world. These were the ninety thousand dollar dredgers, "Am- our" and "Gerber". The Pittsburg Post of March 2, 1914 had headlines..." Dredger "Armour" Finished. Local Ship- builders Set New Mark For Competitors. Largest Clam Shell Ever Built Now Ready For Commission." These two dred- gers were built for the Sutter Basin Improvement Company and had many new and important features built into them. Their hulls were reinforced with structural steel which gave them great durability. The crew compartments were palacial and designed for comfort. The "Armour" had an artificial ice plant and it was the only dredger afloat with that feature. With a 200 foot boom, an eleven ton clamshell operated by a 175 horsepower steam engine, the "Armour" stood in a class by itself.

The "Armour" was first launched on Dec. 7, 1913 and then was finished and commissioned on March 2, 1914. The Pittsburg Post on Dec. 13, 1913 had this story..." Launching of Huge Dredger. Appropriate Ceremonies Attend Event. Mrs. Jean Criswell Littlewood Does Honors By Conferring Title to Monster Vessel... Last Saturday mor- ning the big dredger "Armour" was launched at the Johnson and Lanteri Shipyard and the event was witnessed by a goodly number of persons from San Fransisco, Stockton and other points. Promptly at 10 o'clock the ceremony took place with Mrs. Jean Criswell Littlewood, our clever dram- atic reader, doing the honors of chris- tening the huge vessel.

A. J. Johnson of the shipbuilding firm gave the signal, the guy ropes were flung aside and while the crowd of spectator breathed a silent "Good Luck" the 600 ton hull of the "Armour" glided serenely from the ways into deep water. The only passengers aboard were some forty or fifty skilled laborers to man the craft and effect it's mooring.

The name of "Armour" was given the boat in recognition of one of it's owners, a gentleman well-known in the commercial world. Mr. Armour's favorite color being yellow, all decorations, including the color of the boat, were of that shade.

As a mark of friendly recognition of the occasion the steam whistles at the big Columbia Steel Company's plant were given full blast, followed by a series of short blasts corresponding in number to the letters in the name of Johnson and Lanteri.

Captain L. F. Miller who will have charge of the boat was present."

There was more prose about the launching and size of the "Armour". She was 140 feet in length, 60 feet wide with a water displacement of 14 feet. Her sister ship, "Gerber" was launched several weeks later. Both boats were used to reclaim thousands of acres of swamp and low lands in the vicinity of Knight's Landing, California.

Johnson, Lanteri and three men from Antioch formed the Delta Dredging Company in 1914. A year later the shipyard built the first steel hull hydraulic ditcher, "The Delta No.1" for the new company. Dr. W. S. George and George LaMontagne of Antioch were aboard during it's launching ceremonies and it is possible they were two of the Antioch partners.

Barney Lanteri bought out Johnson's interest in the company in August 1915 and it was the known as Lanteri Shipyard.

The big dredger "Grand Island" was built in 1915. Another dredging vessel "Grand Old Island" was rebuilt for the C. A. Hooper and Company and renamed the "Pittsburg No.1". Hooper owned all the land from Pittsburg to Antioch.

On Sept. 12, 1916 the Contra Costa Gazette had a story that the construction of the new Martinez-Benicia Ferry had been awarded to B. P. Lanteri, the well-known ship builder of Pittsburg. The story said it would be launched in three months, however, it took six months and was launched on March 6, 1917.

The Pittsburg Post had this story....." Ferry Launching. Ceremonies At Pittsburg Tuesday Very Successful...- About 2500 people witnessed the launching of the handsome new ferry steamer "The City of Martinez" at Lantrei's shipyard last Tuesday at 12:30 o'clock. As the boat started to glide down the ways the Pittsburg and grammar school bands played selections, the crowd cheered and whistles blown as Miss Aileen Sanborn of Benicia following the time honored custom broke a bottle of Contra Costa champagne against the boat.

It was the most successful launching ever arranged in the county. In fact, it could not have been better, as Mr. Lanteri had personally arranged every detail and received many congratulations for the manner in which the launching ceremonies were handled as well as upon the construction of such a fine ferry craft. The officers of the Martinez-Benicia Ferry Company expressed themselves as highly pleased with the new boat and were also delighted with the successful launching." The story continued with the speeches of dignitaries.

The new boat was towed to San Fransisco where the engine, boiler and other equipment was installed. Before the vessel could be operated successfully they had to add ballast to the hull so the paddle wheels could reach water. At the time of her construction she was the most modern of ferries. She was 167 feet long with a 54 foot beam. equipped with a 250 horsepower Evans engine and an Eureka oil-burning boiler. Three runways accommodated 40 autombiles. The "City of Martinez" was never noted for beauty but performed her duties until 1936 when she was condemned and burned by the Martinez City Fire Department. The shipyard also built two other ferryboats, the

"Benicia" constructed in 1902 and the "Ramona" in 1913. The "Ramona" was the electric train ferry of the Oakland, Antioch and Eastern Railroad that fell off the ways during launching.

Dredger building was coming to a halt and by 1919 that era was almost over. One of the last dredgers built by Lanteri was the "Neptune" which the hull of the burned out "Grand Island" was used as the foundation of the vessel.

Barney Lanteri was elected mayor of Pittsburg in 1920. His shipyard did not survive his accidental death in 1921 when he died in a boating accident while returning from duck hunting on the Montezuma Slough. His widow sold the shipyard property to the Columbia Steel Company, now the USS-POSCO Industries of Pittsburg.

Some of the shipyard workers in front of office. "Note big mascot dog". The rest of the total number of workers on the next page. From Author's Collection

The rest of Lanteri Shipyard workers. The era was in the early 1900s. From the Author's Collection

Martinez-Benicia ferry boat "City of Martinez" built by Lanteri Shipyard.
March 6, 1917 Launching.

Dredgers under construction. "Note children on building ramp"
From Author's Collection

1910 view of dredgers being built. In the foreground is the "Tule King",
"Alameda" on the shipway and "Monterey" on the right. Dredge beyond is unknown.

View of Johnson & Lanteri Shipyard with the Columbia Steel Mill in the
background. From Author's Collection

WORLD WAR I STARTED A SHIPBUILDING BOOM IN
EAST CONTRA COSTA COUNTY

Early in January 1918, the Daily Ledger had big headlines... "Flag Raising At Shipyard Last Sunday. Important And Pretty Ceremony Attended By 1000 People. Marked Beginning Of An Industry That Will Mean Much To The People Of Antioch...In the presence of an enthusiastic assemblage estimated at least a thousand people, the flag--raising and ground-breaking ceremonies of the Western Shipbuilding Company's yard were held at 2 o'clock Sunday afternoon on the site of the big plant which is soon to be in operation east of town."

The town of Antioch had high hopes for this new company but it never materialized. There were plans to have two ship ways. A short time later the Ledger had a story about the almost completed huge bulkhead of the Western Shipbuilding Company, just east of the town pumping station, that gave way into the river and proved to be almost a complete loss. Nothing more was written about this company except the city council attempted to collect some unpaid bills.

It was very different at Bay Point (later to gain fame as Port Chicago) where the Great Western Shipbuilding Company was located according to a Daily Ledger reporter at the first keel ceremony..."The first keel of one of the ten 9,500 ton vessels for the United States Fleet Corporation was laid with simple ceremonies in the presence of several hundred people. R. N. Burgess, president of the company, and John T. Scott, vice president, had the honor of striking the first blows on the rivets inserted in the plates of the 9,000 ton steamer after keel No.1 in Building Way No.5 had been laid." (the Antioch Daily Ledger reporter made an error as there never was a company by the name of Great Western Shipbuilding Company at Bay Point. The only shipyard was the Pacific Coast Shipbuilding Company). The reason the shipyard was built so far inland at Bay Point was to prevent any damage to ship production should the World War be carried to the West Coast.

John Thomas Scott was a famous marine engineer who designed and built the battleship, "Oregon" and other vessels of note. He was the nephew of Henry Tiffany Scott and Irvin Murray Scott, owners of the Union Iron Works of San Fransisco. This great company built the beautiful yacht, "El Primero" in 1893. So well constructed, it is still sailing in Canadian waters.

John T. and his uncle, Henry T. Scott, were in partnership in the Pacific Coast Shipbuilding Company. It was John's reputation in Washington, D. C. that secured the contract for the 10 ships. John was 96 when he died in March of 1960.

The building of the shipyard was a truly remarkable feat. The construction company of the Lingren Company of San Fransisco built the yard from the bare ground to an enormous plant with 3,500 employees in ninety days. The yard was in use in April, one keel down in May, four keels down and every department running before the end of July. Construction cost was several million dollars. The yard covered 247 acres of land. The plate shed was 400 feet long, the power house was 50 by 100 feet, the blacksmith shop was 50 by 100 feet, the two-story warehouse covered 50 by 100 feet and the office building was 52 by 110 feet.

Trolleys similar to the cable systems used in the Alps were installed on poles 115 feet high and mounted on concrete bases eight feet high. Traveling cranes on the trolleys were used to transport the steel plates from the plate house to the hulls being built on the ways. There were two trolleys for each way. One of the huge dolphins, formed of several piles, used as a stay for the 115 foot aerial masts collapsed. As the mast toppled over, several other masts were knocked down, making a tangled mess of wood, steel ropes and iron. A hundred men escaped being killed or injured as the accident happened at noon while the men were eating lunch. The trolley was repaired and running in a few days.

The facilities of the yard was increased to handle the flow of work and men. Another railroad spur track was built for unloading machinery. The warehouse was increased in size by 100 feet each way. The big company restaurant put in seating to handle 250 more diners and the more modern kitchen equipment. More dormitories were built for singe men.

The great amounts of supplies and materials needed to build the ships can be evidenced by the list of parts received in the first months of operation. The orders were for 100 horizontal cargo winches, 20 capstans, 60 metal life boats and davits, 10 steam windlasses, refrigeration machinery, warping winches, anchors, chains and searchlights. Ninety railroad cars of materials had arrived and 41 were in transit.

The shipyard's 3,500 workers had a permanent committee to handle their personal affairs. The yard's newspaper was named, "Full Speed Ahead". The shipyard had it's own band and it was one of the finest in Contra Costa County. It was called the, "Diablo Band of the Pacific Coast Shipbuilding Company". The band was large with a president, vice president, librarian, business manager and the band master, C. E. Rice. Mr. Rice was a well-known band director.

The Sante Fe and the Antioch, Oakland and Eastern Railroads served the Bay Point area. Workmen from Antioch and Pittsburg used this transportation to the shipyard as the dirt roads were in bad condition most of the time.

The town of Clyde was built as part of the shipyard's program. The property known as the Government Ranch was purchased as a townsite and 103 residences and a large hotel were erected especially to house shipyard employees. However, only 69 of the residences were ever occupied because four special trains brought workers from the Bay cities and waterfront towns. It was cheaper to ride the trains to work than rent the houses. The hotel was a success being filled most of the time and was used for social entertainments having had an excellent ballroom.

The first launching of a vessel was on Nov. 30, 1918. The Ledger had the story..."Launching Of "Diablo" Successful. First Steel Vessel Built In County Takes Water At Bay Point. 5,000 People Witness Ceremony And Enjoy Speeches By R. H. Latimer And Justice Melvin...The launching of the steamship, "Diablo" the first of 10 cargo carriers to be constructed at the yard took place last Saturday and the big hull glided down the ways gracefully exactly at noon. Just as the big steamer started to move, Mrs. R. N. Burgess, following the time-honored custom, broke a bottle of champagne over her bow and christened her "Diablo". The crowd estimated at about 5,000 witnessed the launching and cheered enthusiastically as the vessel received it's first baptism in the waters of the bay. A big banner with the name "Diablo" as well as the flags of the Allied Nations were unfurled and the launching was over."

The story goes on to tell the rest of the launching tale. The whistles and shouts drowned out the music of the band as the hull entered the water of Suisun Bay. Speeches were given by Superior Judge Latimer and State Supreme Court Justice Melvin. A telegram was sent to Mrs. Woodrow Wilson, wife of the U. S. President, thanking her for allowing the vessel's name be changed to "Diablo". The name selected originally by Mrs. Wilson was "Apistama". After the launching, Mrs. Burgess was presented with a bouquet of flowers and a diamond pendant.

The "Diablo" was 416 feet 6 inches long, had a beam of 53 feet, depth of 32 feet. Her speed was 10.5 knots and had a crew of 32. She also had cabins for 4 passengers.

The names selected by Mrs. Wilson for the 10 ships were all of American Indian origin. first was "Apistama" (changed to "Diablo"), second was "Camsunset" and the other names were No.3 "Cockaponset", No.4 "Mohinikis", No.5 "Sinasta", No.6 "Lavada", No.7 "Cuprum", No.8 "Namasket", No.9 "Meanticut" and No.10 "Nashaba" was the last ship built.

The war was over but the shipbuilding company continued constructing the remaining vessels on the U. S. Shipping Board's contract. The company would continue in operation for another 2½ years. On April 5, 1919, the second freighter was launched and according to the reporter it's name was "Sansumet" (that was a misprint as the vessel was "Camsunset").

With 3,500 men working at the shipyard, there was bound to be illegal activities. There were plenty of gambling dens and house of prostitution in Bay Point. One headline had 41 one arrested in a successful raid on several houses. Another big raid Headed by District Attorney A. B. Tinning and Sheriff R. R. Veale, a posse of fifteen officers swooped down on Bay Point at midnight on a Sunday night, closed eight houses of prostitution, arrested a number of women and seized quantities of liquor. At one establishment, run by Peter Manouras, 72 barrels of wine was seized. Numbers of townspeople followed the raiders about and threatened them. When that didn't work, they went ahead and warned proprietors of the houses listed for raiding by the officers.

After 3½ years, the last vessel of the 10 specified by the Government contract was finished. Before this happened there were stories of what was going to happen to the shipyard. One story was that the Delta Oil and Refining Company was going to buy the shipyard. This was pure speculation.

Another headline said... "Shipbuilders May Go To Peru. Report That Bay Point Yards To Be Moved. Officials Neither Confirm Or Deny Rumor. What Will Become Of Clyde? Rushing Work...If present plans carry through, the Paci-

fic Coast Shipbuilding Company upon the completion of "Hull 10", last of it's government contract, will load it's equipment and most of it's work force aboard and make sail for Peru, there to build boats for the Peruvian Government." According to the rest of the story, many of the workers had been called in and offered transportation for them and their families with guarantees for return to the U. S. upon completion of the work in Peru. It said many had accepted and were making arrangements accordingly. The story also said the Navy of Peru at that date consisted of one submarine that wont submerge , and another that they can't get off the bottom, and some ancient surface craft. The rest of the story said the work was being rushed on "Hull 10" and Clyde, one regularly established and modern city, was for sale, cash or terms.

Finally the Ledger had the story of the closing of the yard in June 1921. The headline stated..."Shipyard Closes At Bay Point. Last Of Ten Vessels For Government Finished. All Workers Laid Off...... Hotel At Clyde To Be Closed.... House Rents Reduced." (the house rents at Clyde were reduced from $40 to $20) The story went on to tell the end of work at Bay Point.

The final vessel built by the shipyard was the "Nashaba". In addition to the 10 ships of the Government Contract, two oil tankers were also built by the company.

Since the war ended before the first ship was built at the yard, most of the U. S. Fleet Corporation freighters ended up in storage. This storage area was the mud flats between Bencia and Vallejo. The last ships built by the Pacific Coast Shipbuilding Company were towed directly from Bay Point to the mud flats. Eventually these vessels were sold at a loss to various shipping companies.

The "Cuprum", seventh vessel built by the Pacific Coast Shipbuilding Co. in 1920, was sold to American Mail Line Ltd. in 1927. They renamed her "Shelton" and sold later sold her to the Matson Steamship Company on Feb. 11, 1930. Matson renamed the vessel "Kahuku". While in convoy, during World War II in the Caribbean Sea, she was struck by enemy torpedoes and sunk on June 16, 1942.

The "Diablo", the first ship built, had a long and illustrious career. Although, at first, she had plenty of troubles! On Oct. 12, 1919, sailing from Calcutta, India to San Fransisco, Calif., she was detained at Honolulu with engine troubles. Then, when the "Diablo" was on her way to San Francisco, she ran out of fuel 650 miles from port. Another steamer, "Manoa" towed her to San Fransisco and while there repairs to the vessel's pumps had to be made.

The "Diablo" was sold to many steamship lines and went through many name changes in her lifetime. Matson Steamship Company owned her from 1934 until 1946. During World War II, she was the only vessel in the infamous 35 ship convoy to Murmansk, Russia, that returned to New York in 1942, having been the only ship to escape damage or sunk in that convoy. Upon entering New York Harbor she was struck by lightning! "Diablo" ended her career of 38 years when she foundered (sank) 480 miles southeast of Cape Hatteras on Nov. 3, 1956.

John Thomas Scott designed and built this battleship, "Oregon".

Diablo, the first freighter about to be launched.
From the Contra Costa History Center Collection

Launching of the "Diablo". From the Contra Costa
History Center Collection

Two ships under construction on the ways. "Lavada" in the background. "note the aerial tramways" From the Contra Costa History Center Collection

View of the storerooms and shops. Ship ways in the background.
From the Contra Costa History Center Collection

Pacific Coast Shipbuilding Company, Bay Point, California
From the Contra Costa History Center Collection

Three of the freighters being finished at the Shipyard.
From the Contra Costa History Center Collection

"Diablo" renamed "Maunakea". Photographed in 1944 during
World War II. From the National Maritime Museum Collection

PIGEON RACING HISTORY AND EARLY PIGEON FANCIERS

Pigeon racing goes back to the first ever recording many centuries ago of pigeon or doves (both were one and same). It is the only bird that is the symbol of love and fertility for the Hebrews. The Greeks believe it carried the original source of life

Before 4500 BC, pigeon and doves were kept for bird fighting, for messengers, food, and for war. The homing instincts of the birds made them ideal for sending messages over long distances. How the pigeons manage to find their home loft hasn't been proven and as late as 1936 no solution has been found. As of this date, in my research, I have found no written formula for the phenomenon of the pigeon homing instinct Pigeons will fly hundreds of miles to reach their home loft.

Romans raised pigeons for food, religious purposes and message carrying. A pigeon cote was an important part of their villas and some cotes held 5,000 pigeons.

In Medieval times, every monastery, abbey and manor had a cote to raise pigeons for fresh food during the long winters. It was impossible to keep cattle, sheep and pigs for food during the winter months because of the lack of fodder. The animals not saved for reproduction were killed and the meat salted. This monotonous salt-meat winter diet made fresh pigeon meat a great delicacy. Remember Ole King Cole and his blackbird pie? It was probably pigeon pie.

The early message carrying birds were only capable of flights of about 40 miles. The Caliph of Bagdad in the 12th century maintained a pigeon post, with post offices and postmasters.

By 1819, homing pigeons were developed enough to fly 200 miles or more which was a great distance considering the slow traveling by foot or horse. Reuter's of London made his fortune using pigeons to send information on stock market deals. They were used to fly stock exchange information across the English Channel from European countries.

Roman generals used homing pigeons for military information between army personnel. Pigeons were used for this purpose in later years during the Franco-Prussian War of 1870, World War I, World War II and the Korean War. These homing pigeons weathered severe danger flying in the war zone and many died of injuries from shell and rifle fire after delivering their vital messages to their handlers. Thousands of lives were saved by these birds. Thirty two pigeons in World War I were awarded medals given for heroic action by animals. In World War II, a U. S. homing pigeon called "G. I. Joe," by saving over 1,000 British soldiers, was awarded the Dickin Medal for bravery by the Lord Mayor of London.

Racing of homing pigeons started in Belgium and spread to Holland , then to England. Racing Homer pigeons were imported to the United States shortly after England started their racing programs. By the 1880's, birds in the United States were completing 500 mile races.

The sport and hobby of competition with Racing Homers is popular in most countries and is enjoyed by people in all walks of life. The International Pigeon Racing Federation has 558,559 members and they only raise one breed of pigeon, the Racing Homer. About 40 countries have Racing clubs. It is the hobby of 250,000 persons in England. Even the Queen of England has a loft of racing pigeons. There are over two million people in the world engaged in racing pigeons. The American Racing Pigeon Union, Inc. has a membership of over 20,000 active racers. Disney Land and Disney World USA maintains lofts of white Racing Homers.

There were many people in Antioch, Pittsburg and other towns who were pigeon fanciers. Two of Antioch's pioneers in the late 1800s were avid pigeon racers. Dr. Worth S. George, a distinguished doctor and one of

Antioch's more notable citizens was one. Another was Capt. W. M. Remfree, owner of the Sportsman's Retreat, a barber shop and saloon. The Antioch Ledger in 1896 mentioned their interest in racing pigeons many times. One item had Capt. Remfree flying his birds from San Francisco and Stockton to Antioch. The birds that flew from Stockton made the flight in 35 minutes.

Dr. W. S. George used his Racing Homers for pleasure and business. The Ledger had this story..."Utilizing Homing Pigeons"...Dr. George has a number of homing pigeons. The Doctor is a great man for fads, but this is a fad that promises considerable utility, of which he is developing to be useful. When he has a patient in the country whose case is at all serious, and of whose changing condition he desires periodical reports, without making unnecessary trips, he can utilize his pigeons. He can take a basket of birds and leave them with the family of the patient, and reports as desired are thus returned to him. He has used pigeons with great success in the family of Henry Heidorn. Heidorn's daughter, Miss Emma, has been in precarious condition and the birds with their periodical reports have been a great connivance, for Mr. Heidorn lives several miles from town. He can also have a basket at Somersville, and thus keep track of his patients over there. He is arranging an electrical contrivance so that when a pigeon returns to it's cote with a report he is instantly notified. this will undoubtly prove a great connivance."

Other stories about Doctor George's homing pigeons appeared such as sending a basket of birds out two or three hundred miles to sea, and all found their way home without accident. Another time as a delegate to the Congressional Convention in Vallejo, he sent pigeons to Antioch and kept his friends posted on the proceedings.

One of his birds, "Nelly Bly", won a big race on Sept. 26, 1896 that started from Gilroy, Calif. The Ledger had this to say about his Racing Homer...." One of the most interesting exhibits at the Mechanic's Pavilion was that of the Homing Pigeon, numbering several hundred, and owned by a score of fanciers from different parts of the State. On Wednesday the following card was hung over a demure looking little blue homer..."This Blue Hen, No. 75, W. S. G., won the Mechanics' Institute cup race, from Gilroy, 70 miles distance; average speed per minute 800 yards. Owned by Dr. W. S. George, Antioch, Cal. Two hundred birds competed in the race." Tally one for Antioch."

Doctor George's silver cup known as the "NELLY BLY" Cup, after a long and mysterious journey, is now a prized possession of the Antioch Historical Society.

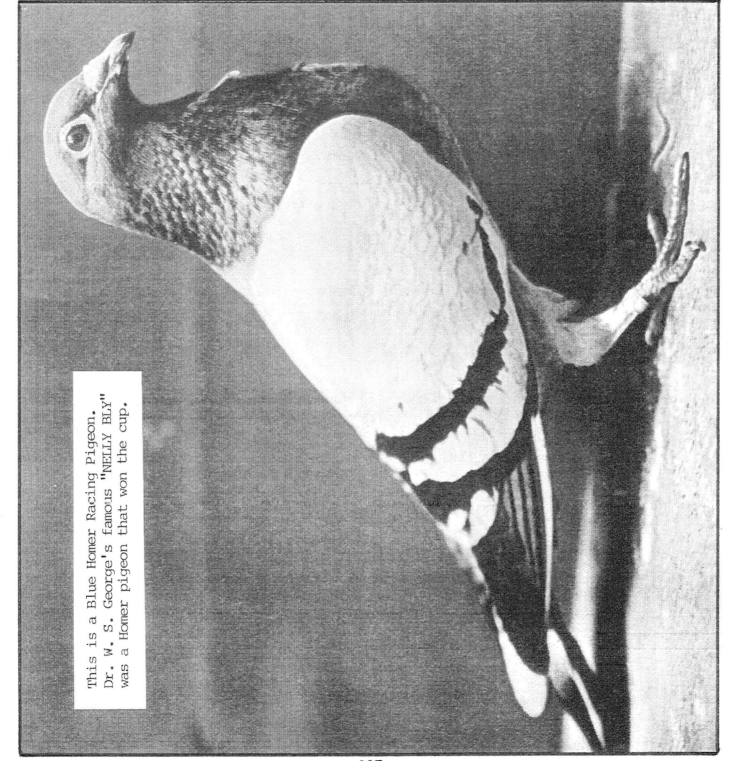

This is a Blue Homer Racing Pigeon.
Dr. W. S. George's famous "NELLY BLY"
was a Homer pigeon that won the cup.

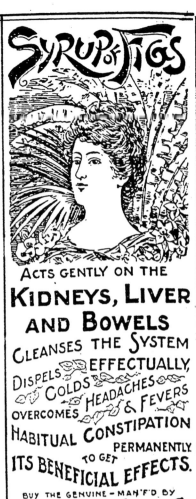

238

DR. WORTH S. GEORGE, PIONEER DOCTOR AND DENTIST

Doctor Worth S. George was born in Armstrong County, Pennsyvania, February 12, 1855. He moved to Monrovia, California in 1885 and later moved to Antioch in 1890. In those early days he was Antioch's physician and dentist. A few years later he opened a drug store on Second Street with Dr. Ratton and Joseph Arata.

Dr. W. S. George in his professional work was exceptional. He would overlook his fees if he felt the family he was treating couldn't afford the expense. Not only did he waive his fees but on many occasions he would supply them with the necessities of life and give a helping hand until they were able to care for themselves. His philosophy was not how much money he could get, but how much good he could do. He worked like this all his life

The doctor liked people who were involved in things and he was a shining example. His life was built on charity, honesty, civic interest and activity and the betterment of his fellow man. Dr. George was extremely active in community in many ways. He was the principal figure in establishing the Methodist Episcopal church and helped build it. When it was finished, he furnished it with an organ and was director of the choir, being an excellent singer.

He organized the first Boy Scouts of Antioch and was the Scoutmaster of the group. When President Teddy Roosevelt stopped in Antioch, George prevailed on him to speak to his scouts. Dr. George was a great admirer of the president.

He was a member of the Antioch School Board and always was a member of any town organization and a firm believer of cooperation in those ventures. He was the medical examiner of many fraternal clubs, the town, insurance companies and the railroads. At one time he was a candidate for the County Coroner but was defeated by only 15 votes.

Doctor George took a very active part in the social life of the town.

He was a charter member of the Eagles, a member of Odd Fellows, Redmen, Moose, Elks Clubs and the Masonic Lodge. His home was always decorated for the holidays. One notice in the Ledger about the 1896 Fourth-of-July Decorations and parade had this to say about his home. "the handsomest residence decoration was that of Dr. George. It was very neat and modest and attracted universal commendation." A photograph of 1912 shows his decorated auto being driven by his wife and her friends in a parade.

The doctor was a proficient hunter and fisherman, always ready to participate in these activities whenever his practice would allow it. Also, He was a crack shot with the rifle, having won many medals while a member of the Antioch Gun Club. He organized and planned many benefits for his Methodist Church and other fraternal and civic organizations.

Typical of his benefits was this one written in the Ledger, "The Novelty Entertainment" Dr. W. S. George covered himself all over with glory with his novelty entertainment. It contained many original and unique characteristics and was indeed a novelty from beginning to end. The doctor is certainly entitled to great credit, for unaided and alone he worked and originated all the features. He is a busy man, has a large professional practice, and to handle an affair of this kind so successfully indicated his administrative ability, for a great amount of labor was involved. One of the pleasant features of the evening was the excellency of the vocal and instrumental numbers. Some of the best local talent participated and this part of the programme was a chaste and elegant treat. It was the first public exhibition of the Doctor's phonograph - graphaphone, and it proved a novelty that was very interesting. This is Edison"s latest and best machine, and said to be the loudest in the world. The doctor was disappointed in not being able to get blank registers, as he intended to give a number of local records. He could, therefore, only give one local record, Assemblyman Belshaw's "Watermillion" song which proved to be one of the best he had. Mr. Belshaw (NOTE: later he was Senator Belshaw) was the same as he is on all occasions as an entertainer.....he captured the house. He was the comedian of the evening in and out of the phonograph. The evening was concluded with music by the Zobo-vocaphone Band. The entertainment was a financial success. The sum of $80 was taken in and the net receipts will be contributed to the M. E. Church. "

Dr. George was well read, a thinker and took great interest in the new things of the world and adapted them for his use. The doctor owned a 1911 Oakland open auto, one of Antioch's first auto owners, and he use to ask young Henry Beede to ride with him and open two gates on the property of The Associated Oil Company's pumping station on Willow Street where one of his patients lived. Henry was nine or ten at the time and although to ride in the auto was exciting, it seemed like a long time setting on the auto's seat waiting for the doctor to return. Dr. George had one of the first radios and he would ask Henry over to his house to listen to the Stanford football games. The doctor's home was on the corner of D and 6th Streets, right across from the Beede home. The doctor was a fancier of Blue Homer racing pigeons and had a cote full of them. One of them, a bird by the name of "Nelly Bly", won a silver cup for taking first place for a race originating in Gilroy, California.

He made unique use of the pigeons to receive word from patients in the country. He would leave homing pigeons at the home of the sick to be released at certain times, bearing messages of the patient's condition. He, also, left baskets of pigeons at Somerville and the coal mines so he could be notified when the doctor was needed there. This method of communication was before there was the telephone and automobiles. Of course, Dr. George had a private telephone system installed at his home before public phones were available.

The doctor somehow found time to have a hobby which was making his property a garden park. His home grounds was filled with plants, flowers and animals. One article in Ledger said " Dr. George, who has been rusticating in the mountains and looking after his mining interests in Sierra county, is back home again. He enjoyed his outing very much. Dr. George brought home from the mountains a pair of beautiful baby deer."

Dr. Worth S. George died suddenly in 1926 from a stroke at the age of 71. He had just returned home from work about six o'clock. The loved and respected doctor died as he would have wished....with a day of good work and a life of good deeds left behind him.

Dr. Worth Scott George, 1902 photo

240

Waving his hat is J. P. Abbott, former State Assemblyman, Dr. Worth Scott George is seated while his brother, Frank George is standing with 1866 Winchester rifle. Seated (l. to r.) are Mrs. Frank George and Mrs. Worth S. George.   Courtesy Antioch Historical Society

Dr. George at the wheel of his 1911 Oakland auto decorated for a parade in Antioch.   From Author's Collection

Dr. Worth Scott George's Antioch home on southeast corner of Sixth and D Streets.   Courtesy Contra Costa County History Center

BRENTWOOD AND BALFOUR-GUTHRIE COMPANY

This story about the early days of the phenomenal, vast farming property of the Balfour-Guthrie Company was accomplished with the reminiscing of Mary Mackenzie Dwelley and Helen Mackenzie Wilson who are the daughters of the second Agent, Alex Mackenzie, of the Company and Charles B. Weeks Jr. whose father was the third man to take charge of the farming property.

Balfour-Guthrie practically rebuilt Brentwood, California to sustain their huge empire. The Bank of Brentwood, the new Brentwood Hotel, the telephone system, the sewage and water systems, new houses and roads were all part of their plans to change the country from dry farming to farming by irrigation. They had bought the Rancho Los Meganos, consisting of 12,700 acres of farm land, from the Savings and Loan Society of San Fransisco for $200,799.43. This was originally Dr. John Marsh's property. The Company purchased the land in April 1910 but did not start the project until February 1913.

Within 13 months Balfour-Guthrie changed Brentwood and completed the vast irrigation district. They then placed 98 tracts or lots ranging in acreage from 5 to 34 acres for sale. All the lands to be watered from the irrigation system and the tracts were sold at $300 per acre, the deed of the property to carry with it a certain number of shares in the irrigation system. The Company then advertised around the world that these unusual and valuable farming properties were for sale. Special trains brought eager buyers from the East and they were housed at the palatial Brentwood Hotel where they were wined and dined by the Company.

Before the huge project was put into being, the area was largely undeveloped and dry farming was practiced. Wheat and barley was grown by this method. If there was a good year with a little rain, a big crop followed. The huge amount of grain from the area was shipped all over the world from Antioch, Port Costa and San Fransisco. The grain crops were gathered by crews using gigantic harvesters drawn by teams consisting of 25 horses. If there was no rain-no crops!.

The main roads were graveled but all other roads were dirt tracks. The farmers made a little extra money hiring out their horse teams to the county to haul gravel in the winter time to repair the main roads. The gravel for this purpose came from Marsh Creek and some was freighted in by railroad cars.

A few farmers had dammed Marsh Creek at one place and practiced irrigation on a very small scale. The Irrigation District established by Balfour-Guthrie changed forever the farming methods of the area and the type of crops that would be grown there. Not everyone was pleased by this transformation of the farming process and there was a lot of resentment against the Company. Many of the established old time farmers were unable to convert from dry farming to irrigated farming and lost their farms due to the high taxes and fees created by the Irrigation District.

The Company's Agent had absolute control over the immense project during the building up of the town of Brentwood and the entire irrigation district. He was also in complete charge after the major part of their plan was finished, such as the sales of the land parcels and their Brentwood Irrigated Farms. He had the power and money to do and/or attempt to implement any scheme or plan that would be of any financial gain for the Company. Balfour-Guthrie picked their most experienced and trusted man for the job. This was Alex Burness, the first Agent in charge of their California Operation. The Company furnished him and his family with a big luxurious house in Brentwood, two expensive open touring cars and servants. There was also formal gardens and gardener to keep it looking beautiful. They didn't pay high salaries but they did supply all the amenities for a comfortable life while working for them.

After the sale of the land parcels, the Company had 13,000 acres left for their Brentwood Irrigated Farms. Alex Burness then had the job of developing this acreage into a paying business and he proceeded to do that. Because a farm of that magnitude required a hundred or more workers to operate it, living quarters and food had to be provided for them. A small city was built on Route 4 just south of Brentwood for the worker's housing.

It consisted of 54 cottages and many tents in this camp and was complete with kitchens, messhalls, showers with hot water, latrines and other up to date advantages. Balfour-Guthrie took good care of their workers but they were also prudent Scotsmen. The messhall dinnerware was fastened on a one foot by twelve foot wood board. Cups were fastened with a chain and the tin plates were nailed down. About ten places were on each board. After the meal, the scrap food was scraped off, the boards were then washed and placed back on the tables ready for the next meal. The workers named this procedure the "Dirty Plate Route".

The food fed to the workers was all grown or raised on the property and was first rate and tasty. Charles Weeks Jr. said the food served consisted of beef, pork, lamb, chicken, milk, cheese, all kinds of vegetables, strawberries, apricots and peaches.

The food scraps from the kitchens and messhalls were taken to the farm's hog ranch and fed to the animals. Nothing was wasted by the management!

Various ethnic workers were hired in the earlier days of the Balfour-- Guthrie's Farms. A tremendous number of Japanese were employed by the Company and they were on the Farms for approximately twenty years. They had their own cooks and the Company had a huge hot tub installed. It was heated by firewood and used by the Japanese men and women for their tradi-

tional hot baths. An area was provided for them to hold their New Year's Celebration. They were excellent workers and a number worked in their native costumes. The Japanese came from Stockton, San Fransisco, Sacramento and Modesto.

Hindus were also hired by other big farms but were considered dangerous by the local people. Alex Mackenzie, the second Agent, was advised to carry a revolver for his protection when he hired Hindus in Imperial Valley. However, he refused to arm himself. Mackenzie was a dark, handsome and six foot tall man and they thought of him a Hindu prince. A considerable number of stories appeared in the Antioch Ledger about fighting among the Hindus and killings in their community. They were employed during the 1920s and were good workers.

Arabs also worked for the Company and there were many of this ethnic group but, according to various persons, they were not well liked. Filipinos were also hired for the farm work but they were not allowed to have women in their camps. It was the condition imposed on the work permits of the Filipinos by law that no women of their country were allowed into the United States. These workers would pool their money and purchase a prestige automobile. After work, ten or more would pile into the shiny car and go for a ride. The driver was the one who could read and speak English and therefore able to pass the state's automobile driver's license examination.

When Alex Burness died in 1921, Balfour-Guthrie brought their Imperial Valley Agent to Brentwood as a replacement. This was Alex Mackenzie who was also the youngest Agent ever hired by the Company, having started with them at twenty-one years of age. Mackenzie, his wife, Betty, two daughters, Mary and Helen first stayed at the Brentwood Hotel and then at one of the Company's cottages until the big mansion was available.

The widow of Alex Burness was allowed all the time needed for the change and to relocate in San Fransisco. She was given all the assistance and help possible by the Company until she made plans for her future. When she moved, the Mackenzies occupied the big mansion.

The Agent's house was in the center of thirteen acres of gardens designed by the famous architect, John McClaren, who planned San Fransisco's Golden Gate Park. He also did the Brentwood Hotel gardens for the Company. A full time gardener attended to the Agent's gardens which consisted of the ornamental garden and vegetable garden and a vineyard. Mackenzie would grow experimental row crop vegetables in his garden even when his gardener insisted they wouldn't grow in that type of soil. The successfully grown vegetable was then planted in the big fields for production. Mackenzie's son, John, was born at the big house.

Mackenzie finally sold this big house and the showplace grounds as he said he was sent to Brentwood to make money, not spend it. The family moved into the big house on Walnut Blvd. that had been built for the head engineer of the Irrigation Project. Mary Dwelley said the city should have bought the 13 acres for a city park because of it's great beauty.

When Alex Mackenzie needed an assistant he hired Charles B. Weeks Sr. from an ad in agricultural magazine. Weeks was born in Kinsley, Kansas and was living in Red Bluff, California before moving to Brentwood. In 1916 he was in the army and had fought during the Mexican War. He was first hired by the Kirkwood Nurseries and worked there during the year of 1921. Weeks went to work for Mackenzie and Balfour-Guthrie in 1922 and was very good at his job. He worked with Mr. Kirkman who was in charge of planting the huge orchards for the Company. Kirkman was a man with great vision about the value of the orchards in the future. However, he was not to well liked as he was a penny-pinching and wordy man. He wouldn't pay his

help if he could get away with it. Kenneth Dwelley remembered at the age of 11 or 12 years he worked for Kirkman, irrigating the orchards during the summer. He worked 15 hours a day for 15 cents an hour. Kirkman would not pay the young boy at the summer's end until he was confronted by Kenneth's father.

Apricot, peach, nectarine and many other types of fruit and various nut trees were planted. The orchards covered land from Brentwood to Marsh Creek. A company engineer laid out the orchards only to find a mistake had been made in the plans. The water from the irrigation lines wouldn't flow the right way and the orchard layout had to be changed so the system would operate properly.

The vast farm's big dairy with it's foreman's residence was located on Walnut Blvd. After the orchards were started there was a great deal of acreage still unused so the cattle were turned loose to graze. The milk from the cows was very rich and the dairy had a cooling room for the milk. Young Junior Weeks relished drinking a cool glass of milk off the cooling bars.

Besides the dairy, there was the hog and sheep ranch, the horse ranch with it's great equipment barns and horse barns that were on Concord Ave. The blacksmith's shop was also on the horse ranch. Nise, the smith, could shoe the two ton horses without any trouble. Each of the ranches had a large house for the foremen and their families. All houses were completely furnished by the Company. There was a total of 10 farms or ranches in the Brentwood Irrigated Farms.

When grass was grazed out by the vast flocks of sheep, they were moved from the Brentwood area through Vasco to back of the Livermore hills to new pastures. Charles Weeks Jr. remembered making this trip at eight years of age. The first night stop was at Byron and the second night was at a bridge. The third night was at ranch near Livermore and this was as far as Junior was allowed to travel with the flocks. From there he was sent back home with one of the sheepherders. The pastures back of the Livermore hills were lush with grass and when the sheep returned to Brentwood they were fat. The sandy land of the sheep ranch by the old Marsh House made an excellent place for the ewes to have their lambs. Mackenzie brought abandoned lambs, whose mothers had died, home for the children to raise. An article in the local newspaper on March 8, 1927 said Balfour-Guthrie, one of the largest local sheep growers sheared 40 bales of wool (each one weighing 300 pounds) from their flocks. The wool was sold to the Pacific Co-op Wool Growers.

Alex Mackenzie died in 1929 at the age of 42 of meningitis contracted while on one of his trips checking on the Company's holdings in the Imperial Valley. His wife, Betty, followed him in death three years later. The three children had a guardian, Ulrich Karrer, who watched over them until they were of age or married. Balfour-Guthrie furnished financial aid during this crisis. Kenneth Dwelley, of Dwelley Farms, and Mary were married in 1939, Helen married an attorney, John Wilson and John Mackenzie is a retired newspaper journalist and a publisher of newsletters for organizations of retirees.

Charles B. Weeks Sr. was appointed general manager of Balfour-Guthrie and the Brentwood Irrigated Farms after MacKenzie's death. He held that position with them and succeeding owners from 1929 until 1970 when he retired. It is interesting to note that the office of Agent was not conferred on Weeks. However, he proved to be an outstanding agriculturist and administrator and as such he made Brentwood Irrigated Farms an extremely profitable property for the Company.

Weeks was a man that was interested in what happened in the community and was deeply involved in the local politics. He was one of the founders of the Brentwood Lions Club, a Mason, president of the California Grape and Fruit Tree League, president of the Brentwood Fire Commission, president of the East Contra Costa Irrigation District, a trustee of the Brentwood Union School District, a member of the County Housing Authority and a member of many other organizations. A man that gave back a lot to the community. Weeks was also an avid amateur photographer and captured much of the history of the area on film. An interesting note, to be on the Board of Directors of the Irrigation District you must own property and Weeks had none so Balfour-Guthrie deeded the property on Walnut Blvd. that included the chief engineer's big house to him. That way he became a director.

Weeks was always involved in innovative farming practices and he was always the first to try something new. He designed the farms' pesticide sprayers and had them built. When aircraft was first used for this purpose, he had them on the farms spraying the orchards. Three beautiful high-wing cabin monoplanes were built in Stockton by the Hawke Aircraft Company expressively for pesticide spraying. Weeks used them on the farms. There was a news clip of April 1933 that said..."Two planes of the Hawke Dusting Company have been busy working over the orchards of Bentwood the past two days." He was also very good at doctoring sick animals and the veterinarian was seldom called to the farms.

Until the orchards were developed enough to produce fruit, Charles Weeks Sr. decided to plant row crops on the unused land with sugar beets, tomatoes and cucumbers. He planted twenty acres of cucumbers. They grew so fast and were so numerous, more help had to be hired to pick them. The Company cannery was swamped by the time the second pickings arrived. They had to stop picking until the cannery caught up with the cucumbers. It usually took six pickings to clear the field of cucumbers.

Tomatoes were difficult and time consuming to grow. Seeds were planted in frames. When the seedlings were so high they were transferred to a second frame and the procedure was repeated with a third frame. During this time the plants were kept warm with lanterns. When the tomatoes reached the desired height, they were planted in rows six feet apart. The Japanese workers were used and they enjoyed this type of farming. However, it was to expensive to grow the tomatoes with this method and Balfour-Guthrie stopped growing them after several seasons.

Balfour-Guthrie's drying shed and drying field for apricots was the largest in the world. The drying field was located south of Brentwood near the worker's camp on Hwy 4. Their packing shed for fruits was located in Brentwood across from the Brentwood hotel and beside the railroad tracks. It was a city block long and two stories high. After it was built, the Company moved their offices from the hotel into the second story of the packing shed. In 1937 Balfour-Guthrie built a precooling plant in the shed that was designed to be the most modern and efficient fruit handling system ever built. The Pacific Ice Company that installed the precooler also built an ice plant across the road from the packing shed. It was mechanically refrigerated and used for train car icing and precooling for other shippers.

During the harvest season, the packing shed was a beehive of activity. Men, women and children all worked with a frenzy. The work started at six o'clock in the morning and lasted late into the night ending at ten or eleven P.M. The trucks arrived at the shed with the lugs of fruit which were dumped on conveyer belts where workers sorted the unusable fruit from the choice fruit. The packers filled the shipping boxes with neat rows of the fruit. The boxes were manufactured in the box factory upstairs in the packing shed. They were sent down on an overhead conveyer belt. The girls stamped the date on the filled boxes and sent them on a conveyer to the tally persons who counted the boxes as they were loaded into the freight cars. Later when the precooling plant came into operation, the boxes of fruit stayed in that part of the shed for a short period of time before being loaded into the cars.

The Farm's hog and sheep operation was dismantled during a drought year in the 1920's and the hogs and sheep were sold off. The dairy farm met the same fate when the new government rules and regulations made the operation unprofitable for the Company and it was sold.

By 1931, a big change in the agricultural labor became evident. Local farmers were hired to till the land but the huge volume of fruit being produced in the orchards required a great number of fruit pickers. The Company hired all the local people but more help was needed. The Great Depression found many farmers, living in the Midwest with no income, loading up their cars and trucks with their families and household goods. They headed for California. Many found work on the Balfour-Guthrie Farms, working for 15 to 17 cents an hour. The Dust Bowl disaster in Oklahoma and Texas in 1934 forced many more farmers to migrate to California and the work force overwhelmed the Brentwood area. Many hundreds of workers were not hired and the broke and discouraged men and their families lived in tent camps on vacant land and railroad right-of-ways without sanitation and water.

Virginia Winter remembered in an article she wrote for the Brentwood News how her family moved to Brentwood in 1936 after losing their farm in South Dakota. Her father bought a second hand sedan in good condition. They loaded the back seat with clothes, blankets, pillows, photo snapshots and food. Twelve year old Virginia sat atop of everything. When they reached Brentwood, they moved into an unused old milk shed on Bixler Road and they furnished it with folding cots, lug boxes, boards and a kerosene camp stove. Later they moved to a two room cabin on Hwy 4 north of Brentwood. Mr. Winter found work here and there. He eventually bought an inexpensive lot and built a small house after finding year-round work on the Farms. Many of the transients settled down in the Brentwood area.

Balfour-Guthrie gave two big parties a year. One was the May Day Party and Barbecue. A special chef was brought in to prepare the thick steaks, pork and chicken. At Christmas, a Company truck was sent up to the hills and the Christmas tree was selected and cut for the occasion. It was placed in the Cafeteria and then decorated by everyone in the camp. The Christmas dinner was served with every kind of festive food. Each worker received a large Christmas stocking filled with oranges, apples and hard candy. The Company paid for these parties for many years.

By 1934 registration of migratory workers became a part of the State Employment Service in combination with the Federal Agencies. The laborers were systematized by methods that speeded up the movement of workers from one area to another in the state during the harvesting season. The Social Security setup was part of the Federal involvement. The Brentwood branch of the Employment Service registered 3800 workers in 1936 and 4217 in 1937. The wages had increased from 15 cents to 40 cents an hour. There was also much labor unrest and the labor unions attempted to organize the laborers in the area. However, Balfour-Guthrie's Farms had no trouble with their workers and they crossed the picket lines to work for the Company. The overcrowding of the permanent labor camps during the harvest season caused the Resettlement Administration in California to launch a program of a series of model camps for migra-

tory workers. In 1942, the National Defense Housing Administration gave priority for a mobile camp for fruit workers in Brentwood. Charles B. Weeks Sr. announced the camp would be located northwest of Brentwood and would be reached from Lone Tree Way or Oakley Highway.

When the mobile camp was installed it housed 200 workers and their families in floored tents. It was run like a city with a mayor and a council. The camp was complete with power units, shower baths, laundry, library, kitchens, assembly tent, a nurse with a hospital van and an employment office. The camp remained at this site until after the apricot and peach harvest season. It was then moved to another harvest site in the state.

There was a big annual event started in 1926 known as the Apricot Festival celebrating the harvest of the apricots. It was held in the City Park with a reigning queen. There was a huge parade with floats, decorated autos and wagons, many bands, horses and riders and marching groups. Dances and picnics were part of the program and a carnival was set up on the Park grounds. Again Weeks was a prominent part of this event. the Festivals lasted until 1937 when the East Contra Costa Chamber of Commerce withdrew their support. It was claimed the growers opposed having the Festival during the harvesting season. They said the harvesting was more important and the work was interrupted by the event. Also labor unrest was mentioned, plus the owners blamed a rowdy element for the disorder and violence that occurred during the Festival.

Brentwood Irrigated Farms was one of the largest operations in this state and they introduced scientific farming. They grew immense tonnage of crops such as squash, cucumbers, pumpkins, melons, beans, wheat, barley, peaches, plums, apricots, walnuts, tomatoes and other vegetables, fruit and nuts. During World War II the Farms increased their production to meet the demands of the war effort.

In 1942, all the products shipped from Diablo Valley would have filled a train 18½ miles long or one whose engine would be past Pittsburg before the caboose rolled out of Brentwood. Perishable products, vegetables and fruit, filled 1174 railroad cars.

The size of the Balfour-Guthrie organization in the world was huge. Among it's many operations was their shipping line that they used to ship their products around the world. When World War II broke out, the very first vessel to be torpedoed by a submarine was one of Balfour-Guthrie's fleet of freighters.

The Brentwood Irrigated Farms continued operation until 1950 or 1951 when they were acquired by the Western Fruit Grower's Company of Los Angles, Calif. They in turn sold the property to Thomas and Phil Davis, two attorneys from Stockton. The Davis brothers finally sold off the Farms, piece by piece, and relocated their agriculture operation in the southern part of the state. This ended the Brentwood Irrigated Farms. Charles B. Weeks Sr. managed The Davis property until his retirement in 1970.

Note...All photographs illustrating this story are from the Charles B. Weeks Jr. Collection.

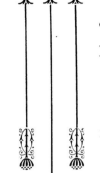

New Brentwood Hotel under construction. Old Brentwood
Hotel razed at this site. 1913

Court area of new Brentwood Hotel.

Lobby and registration desk of the hotel.

Large elaborate Dining room with crystal table settings.

HOTEL BRENTWOOD

¶ ANNOUNCEMENT
is made that the
NEW HOTEL AT
BRENTWOOD
WILL BE OPENED ON
Monday, December 1st, 1913

¶ DINNER WILL BE SERVED AT 6 P. M. $1.00 PER PLATE.

¶ FOR TABLE RESERVATIONS ADDRESS

A. C. REYNOLDS, Manager

The finished Brentwood Hotel. Balfour-Guthrie owners.

252

Brentwood bank built by Balfour-Guthrie.

Brun Bros. Brentwood Garage built by Ferd Stamm.

The source of water for East Contra Costa Irrigation Co.
Indian Creek, A branch of San Joaquin River.

Excavating the main irrigation canal at the west end
of dredged Indian Slough canal.

Main Canal and Pump Station

Main irrigation canal and No, 1 pump Station.

Interior of one of the Pump Stations.

255

House built for chief Engineer. Later deeded to Charles Weeks.

Home built for Balfour-Guthrie Agent. One of his two autos.

Marsh Creek Road with Marsh House in background.

One of Balfour-Guthrie farms on Marsh Creek road.

Balfour-Guthrie chichen ranch supplied eggs and meat.

Balfour-Guthrie herd of cattle that supplied milk, butter and beef for their workers.

Farm officials inspecting waist-high wheat in one of their fields.

Workers picking fruit in one of Balfour-Guthrie orchards.

Bags of beans ready for shipment

Plowing the field with a huge plow pulled by one of the Track Layers.

This is one of the mammoth Track-Layer tractors. Tank tracks on back moved the tractor and it was steered by the single big wheel in front.

Alex. Mackenzie, Second Agent of Balfour-Guthrie Company. Photo courtesy of his Daughter, Mary Mackenzie Dwelly

An early crop-dusting airplane used by Balfoiur-Guthrie.

Hawk Aircraft No. 3. One of three crop dusting Hawks
built in Stockton for use on Balfour-Guthrie Farms.

Children also worked during the apricot season.

Busy Balfour-Guthrie packing shed during apricot season.

One of the Track-Layers towing six wagon loads of produce

Workmen loading racks of sun dried apricots. Balfour-Guthrie
Co. had one of the world's largest fruit drying operations

ANN NOIA HENRY AND HER DAUGHTERS SAILED THE SEAS IN 1918

The Daily Ledger had the story of the church wedding of Anna Noia and Captain Joseph P. Henry in the October 11, 1913 issue of the paper. Anna Noia was an extraordinary woman who was adventurous and far ahead of the women of her time.

She was a lovely girl, born in Antioch, and she lived in the southeast part of the town. The Noia home is still in existence and is located on Noia Avenue, although it has been modified so many times as to be almost unrecognizable.

Captain Henry was the master of the wooden four masted schooner, "Henry Wilson", owned by the North Alaska Salmon Company. The vessel was built in 1899 by the shipbuilder, J. Lindstrom in Aberdeen, Wash. It was 157.8 feet long, 37.1 feet wide and drew 11.3 feet of water.

In 1912, Capt. Henry sailed the "Henry Wilson" to Antioch from Alameda and the vessel spent several months at anchor here. Many vessels were brought to Antioch to rid the bottom of barnacles in the fresh water of the river and this was probably the reason the "Henry Wilson" was here.

The story told by relatives indicate Anna met Joseph at an Antioch dance at this time and that was when their romance began, which culminated with their marriage on October 5, 1913. They were married at the old Catholic Church on G Street by Father E. Lawrence.

The young people left on the Southern Pacific train for a honeymoon in Los Angeles. Upon their return made their home in Oakland.

Captain Henry made regular trips to the Alaska fishing waters for his company and was one of the best known and popular sailing men in the bay region.

To get a better idea of Anna's courage, some of the Alaska Packers Association's history is necessary. Fishing and canning of salmon began in San Fransisco bay and on the Sacramento and San Joaquin Rivers. Much of this was done in Pittsburg and Antioch.

When salmon became scarce, the fishing moved north to the Columbia River in 1866, British Columbia by 1875 and then to Alaska several years later.

In 1893, several independent fishing firms, located in the San Fransisco area, led by Henry Fortman merged to create the largest salmon packing company in the world...the Alaska Packers Association.

The employer of Henry was one of the merging firms. By 1916, the peak of the company's fleet, there were 93 vessels flying red-and-black APA house flag. All of their ships were purchased second hand and then modified to do the salmon fishing business. There were 16 iron and steel sailing ships, part of their famed "Star" fleet. These vessels were renamed as "Star of Alaska", "Star of India", "Star of Bengal", etc.

There was nine wooden sailing ships, including the "Henry Wilson", and sixty eight steamers, towboats and launches. The Packers owned 14 canneries in Alaska and two on Puget Sound. They also owned two salmon hatcheries. During the winter months the fleet stayed at the 77 acres of Alameda waterfront owned by the APA.

In April or May, the fleet would embark on the 2500 mile journey to the Alaskan waters for the fishing season and return in late August or September with their holds crammed full of canned salmon.

Sailing and fishing in the Bering Sea and the Alaskan waters was bitter cold work. The Packers suffered losses in the gale tossed waters and storms with sunken ships. Their worst loss was the "Star of Bengal" who dragged her anchors in a gale and went aground on Coronation Island off southeast Alaska with the loss of 110 lives.

Other ships were crushed in the ice and sank...it was very easy to be trapped in the ice.

Fishermen/sailors received a total of 25 dollars for sailing the ship to Alaska and back, Captain Joseph

Henry's salary was $180 for a month. While fishing in the two-man gill-net boat, the men received 2¢ per fish caught.

1917 was the worst year for gales in Bristol Bay with large numbers of fishing boats driven ashore.

Anna's story begins in 1917 and is recorded in her log of the voyage to Alaska on the "Henry Wilson" with her husband and their two young children, Blanche and Thelma. The United States was at war with Germany which makes the story even more interesting.

This was the second trip the captain had taken his wife and children along. The first trip was to Japan and the Philippine Islands.

This voyage was from Tacoma, Wash. to Sidney and Newcastle, Australia and from there to Bristol Bay, Alaska and then back to Seattle, Wash. and, finally, on to San Fransisco, Calif. They were at sea a total of 173 days.

The "Henry Wilson" set out to sea with eight crewmen, a couple of cats and a dog on Dec 4, 1917 from Tacoma and this was the start of Anna's log. Normally the fishing fleet sailed for Alaska in the Spring, however, the "Henry Wilson" was to pick up a cargo of coal at Newcastle for the Alaskan canneries' boilers.

They ran into bad weather the first day out and Anna wrote in her log.."Dec 6, In a big sea and a big blow and talk about a tuss! Joe says getting out of Flattery is something like getting around Cape Horn. Myself and two kids seasick. Thelma scared to death and would creep around." Then they had many days of good weather and she wrote about the type of meals they ate and she read books and they fished.

On Dec 24, she wrote..."In a dead calm. Hot as blazes. Been fixing the kids Christmas tree. We perspire from morning till night. 7.30 P.M. Xmas Eve, Joe dressed up like Santa Claus and scared the life out of the kids. " Dec 25..."Xmas Day. Almost in a calm yet. Been playing the victrola most all morning. Had canned roast meat, with creamed carrots, succotash, beans, plum pudding, fruit cake and lime juice."

On Dec. 27 one of the cats was missing and was presumed lost overboard. At this time of the voyage they were close to the Equator and the weather was so hot the pitch was boiling out of the deck seams. All kinds of fish in the hundreds were seen from the deck and the crew caught many of them for their dinners.

Because of the war situation, the "Henry Wilson" ran without lights and each time they saw an island, Blanche would ask if it was German.

Somewhere near the South Sea Islands the deck became covered with pumice and the sea full of ashes. It probably was from an undersea volcanic disturbance. On Feb. 14, the vessel was caught in a cyclone and Thelma was creeping around as she couldn't stand up on account of the rough weather and Anna said..."The sea was mountains high. Joe had to put out oil bags to help calm the water around the boat."

They reached Sidney on Feb. 19 and were towed in to the dock. There they had mail from home, three letters and a couple of Antioch Ledgers. Anna said in her log that they stayed in the best hotel in Australia, the Hotel Australia, for four days and during that time they visited with friends and saw much of the city. The vessel was fumigated and they also had a painting of the "Henry Wilson" done on canvas while in Sidney. Parties were held on the ship to entertain friends and officials.

On March 10 they sailed to Newcastle, arriving there on March 11 and started to load the coal cargo. With the cargo aboard they left on March 13 for Alaska and another cyclone hit them and Anna was seasick for three days. She wrote..."during the storm, Joe stayed outside most of the time from 4 A.M. till late at night, His face was covered with salt from the spray. He double reefed the sails and tied the wheel down so there was no man at the wheel. We only waited for the storm to get over. The sea was mountains high."

By April the ship's crew was starting to see ice floes in the water. On April 11 they were in a dead calm for a week and during this time they went fishing in the ship's launch. Joe took Blanche fishing one day and a shark bit the propeller stopping the launch so he went back to the ship, got a rifle and harpoon...he and a sailor killed 11 sharks in three hours.

On April 26, a troublesome crew member, by the name of Murphy, dropped a new paint scraper overboard on purpose and then got sassy about it according to Anna's log. The Captain handcuffed him and put him in the brig. She said on May 1..."Murphy was out of prison again as he was willing to work."

On May 12, Anna's log had this written..."Joe made a steam pump as the boat is leaking some. The mates and sailors said it was impossible for him to make it but he made a dandy one. Good weather and a fine breeze." Then on May 20, she wrote... "In a calm. Joe found the leak in the boat. He and the carpenter went out in the launch so as to be able to fix it, and as Joe had his hands near the water edge, a shark came up and nearly caught his arm. He killed it with the rifle a few minutes later."

By June 8, they had weathered another gale and heavy fog with another big blow and high seas. Also on June 8 was the eclipse of the sun from 8:30 A.M. till 11 o'clock. They were now 130 miles from Unimak Pass in the Aleutian Islands.

On June 12, they went from the Pacific Ocean though the Pass into the Bering Sea. She said it was quite cold and all the hills and mountains were covered with snow. It was daylight till 10 P.M. and again at 2 A.M. She had trouble getting the children to go to bed at night. On June 15, Anna wrote about all the ice around the boat and how strange it was to see

it this late in the year. The ship made slow passage through the ice packs the next few days. The "Henry Wilson" finally got into really dangerous ice and wasn't able to push through it and Joe had to turn back toward Port Hayden. Anna said they made some ice cream and filled their water tanks with the ice as it was fresh water ice.

On June 20, they arrived at Bristol Bay, Alaska and she wrote that vessels, "J. B. Hunt" and "Star of France" were aground on the shore. There were quite a few vessels in the harbor. The "Tacoma" went to pieces in the ice and some men lost their lives there in the harbor. The same ice forced the other two ships aground. She said later that they got the two ships off the mud flats.

"Henry Wilson" was anchored near the town of Naknek. Mail arrived including issues of the Ledger. Also Anna received a surprise bouquet of flowers from her parents in Antioch and she pressed some blossoms in her log.

The crew was kept busy sending lighters of coal ashore for the two canneries operating at Naknek. Their friends on other vessels and the canneries sent special foods and candies over for Anna and the children. The captain was still having trouble with Murphy and he was back in the brig again.

Joe moved the ship to where the fishing was in progress and Anna wrote of seeing about 600 of the two-- man gill-net boats all catching fish. Lighters were filled with the fish and towed to the canneries. She said she saw one lighter with the crew throwing overboard a thousand fish because the canneries were so busy they could not keep up with loads of fish.

Sometimes lighters would sink from being overloaded with fish. In the bad weather, the crews would have to dump fish to keep afloat. Each lighter sunk was a loss of $14,00-0.00 and there were losses. Anna said

269

the superintendent of the canneries was upset about the loss of fish and the lighters.

By July 18, the fish was getting scarce. Joe had salted several barrels of salmon to take back to Oakland. They entertained guests aboard the "Henry Wilson" and visited other ships and the cannery foremen's homes.

By the end of July they set sail for Dutch Harbor and the voyage home. They stopped at Port Moeller on the way as the weather was bad. Anna said there was the big cannery, 2 dozen houses and a big store. She bought dress goods, cards, underwear, gum, shells, candy and other small things at the store.

They reached Dutch Harbor located on Unalaska Island in the Aleutian Islands on Aug. 4 after a rough trip. The "Henry Wilson" was loaded with 12,000 cases of salmon for the trip back. A Fred Crown and family came aboard and they were making the trip back to the States with them. The ship was ready to sail to Seattle and Tacoma on Aug. 17. Anna's log said the day before they left the mail boat, "Dora" went on the rocks and she guessed they wouldn't get any mail before they left.

On Aug. 29, her log said they made 264 miles in 24 hours and they were 600 miles from Unimak Pass and had 900 miles more to go before reaching Seattle. The crew was starting to clean the paint work. On Sept. 4, they were in a dead calm and Anna's log said..."Been in a dead calm all day The sun shone this afternoon, gosh, it was a hot sun though. I finished some sewing this afternoon. Joe caught two gouneys and put them on deck and "Bum" the big dog went for the gouneys...but the gouney fought to beat the band and the dog couldn't get him. As soon as they get on board they get sea-sick and can hardly walk. Finally Joe took off his cap and while the gouney was trying to peck at his cap, Joe caught him by the neck and put him over the side again. Everybody was excited but it was real fun for

a few moments." (With the help of the Lindsey Museum in Walnut Creek, the gouney was identified as an alba-tross.)

The next day a whale got close to the vessel and Joe shot at it with his rifle.

On Sept. 11, they sighted the Cape Flattery light ship near British Columbia and Washington State. They anchored the ship at Neah Bay on Sept. 12 where Joe went ashore and called for a tug to tow the vessel through the strait and Puget Sound to Seattle. The tug "Prosper" picked the ship up on Sept. 13 and had them at the Watcom Street Wharf on the following day. The next day they were towed to Tacoma where the cargo of canned salmon was discharged. Anna and her family spent several days enjoying the city of Tacoma.

The last entry in her log was Sept. 21, 1918 and it said..."Think we will leave for "Frisco" on Monday. The skylights are being repaired." and so ended Anna Noia Henry's adventurous voyage.

Some of the other entries in her log described how they had canvas lining the rails to keep the children from falling overboard. Her visits to the Eskimo villages. The beauty of the snow covered mountains and land. How she read books, made dresses for her and the children. Watched whaling ships chasing whales.

Not many women in her era would embark on such a journey with two very small children.

Only two ships of the Alaska Packers Association's huge fleet survive today. The "Star of Alaska" now known by her original name of "Balclutha", is restored and is part of the Maritine Museum fleet moored at San Fransisco. The other one is the "Star of India", restored and moored at San Diego.

Capt. Joseph P. Henry with Anna and daughters. 1920
From the Henry's Collection

Capt. Joseph and Anna's wedding photograph. 1913

Rose and Anna Noia. Anna made the dresses and Rose made the hats.
While on the voyage, Anna sewed clothes for her daughters and herself.
From the Henry's Collection

Second Mate and Capt. Joe Henry. Because the mate was taller than Henry he was on a seat. From the Henry's Collection

Noia Family and home on Noia Ave. 1908 From Author's Collection

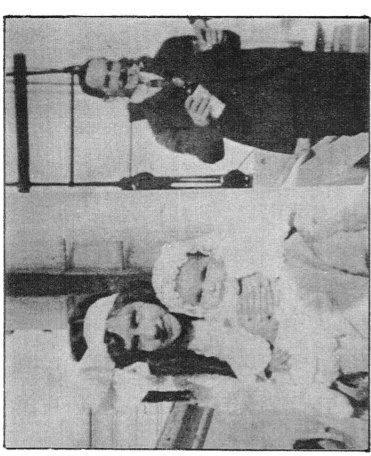

Blanche's Christening Day celebration
aboard the "Henry Wilson".

Anna's family on deck of "Henry Wilson"

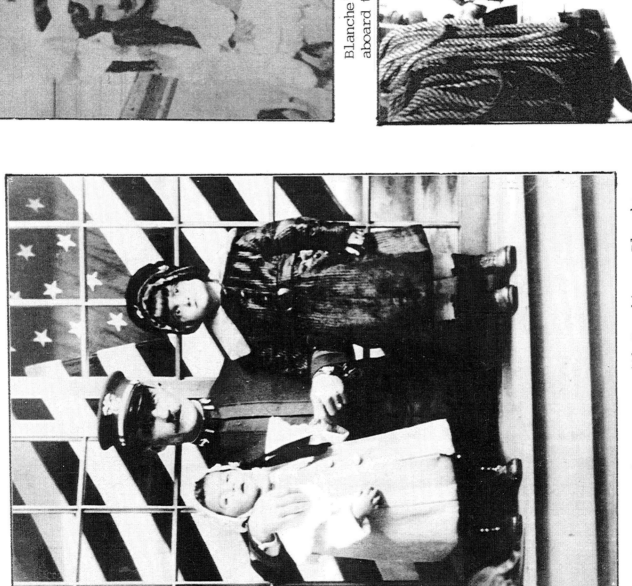

Navy Lieut. Joseph P. Henry with Daughters, Blanche
and Thelma. Photo taken just before the voyage.
From the Henry's Collection

274

Captain Henry at work aboard the "Henry Wilson" during the voyage. From the Henry's Collection

Thelma and Blanche aboard the "Henry Wilson". From the Henry's Collection

Blanche, Anna and Thelma on the deck From the Henry Collection

Capt. Young with sextant–died in Alaska. Jerry Murphy
was strangled in S.F. Murphy is the big fellow.

Barkatine "Fearless" Both ships were in Manila
same time as the "Henry Wilson".

Barkatine "Echo" in Manila Bay

SHIP ST. FRANCIS, ON THE ROCKS. ALASKA.

Ship "St. Francis" on the rocks in Alaska

Gouney bird. Some times called "dead sailor's souls" Caught at sea.

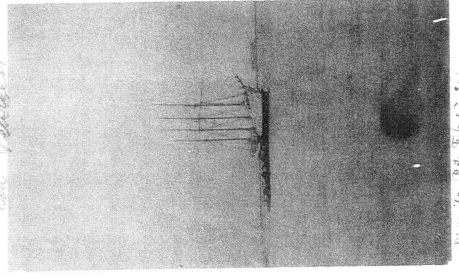

Ship "Fearless" in Manila bay February 13, 1917

Shark 1918. Eleven of these harpooned and shot in three hours for fun.

Captions on these two pages of photographs taken during the voyage are Anna's

Four masted schooner, "Henry Wilson" preparing to unload cargo of cases of salmon at San Pedro, Calif. From the National Maritime Museum

Painting of the schooner "Henry Wilson" that was done in Sidney, Australia
From the Henry Collection

What Every Woman Should Know

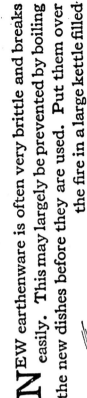

THE old method of toasting bread by using a fork usually results in toasting the hands and face of the cook. Besides this discomfort, it is difficult to obtain an even brown color, the edges of the slice of bread often being burnt while the center is still uncooked. By using the New Perfection Toaster, four slices of bread can be toasted at one time, and all will be toasted exactly alike.

NEW earthenware is often very brittle and breaks easily. This may largely be prevented by boiling the new dishes before they are used. Put them over the fire in a large kettle filled with cold water. Bring to boiling point slowly and boil briskly for a minute. Let the earthenware cool before taking out of the water. Lamp chimneys and other pressed glassware may be treated in the same manner. Cut glass, however, should never be put into either very hot or cold water.

What Every Woman Should Know

AN embroidery frame may be used to great advantage when mending underwear or three-cornered tears. Carefully press the mended spot to obtain the best results.

TO clean white enamelled woodwork try sweet milk and ammonia.

This mixture may be made at home in the proportions of two tablespoonfuls of ammonia to a quart of milk. This will not turn the enamel yellow, as certain kinds of soap are apt to do.

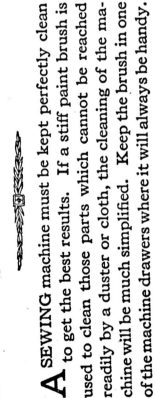

A SEWING machine must be kept perfectly clean to get the best results. If a stiff paint brush is used to clean those parts which cannot be reached readily by a duster or cloth, the cleaning of the machine will be much simplified. Keep the brush in one of the machine drawers where it will always be handy.

IT is quite difficult to dry lace curtains without a stretcher. However, it can be done by laying a clean sheet on the floor of a room not in use, and stretching the curtains upon it carefully, sticking a pin through each point of the lace.

ROOSEVELT JUBILEE CELEBRATION

One of the biggest events ever to happen in Antioch was the spectacular week long Roosevelt Jubilee. It was the brainchild of Bragdon R. Garrow, a man with civic pride and an outstanding business man. Garrow had many ideas and far reaching visions for Antioch. When he couldn't convince the city that the downtown needed change to meet the growing needs of the community's purchasing power, he built the Antioch's first shopping mall in 1968. The County East Shopping Mall was built several miles from the downtown and it became the premier shopping area for residents.

The event was planned 48 hours after the March 4, 1933 inauguration of the new president, Franklin D. Roosevelt. Antioch "live wires" headed by Garrow decided that Antioch would be the first city in the nation to stage a Roosevelt Jubilee.

A letter was sent to Walter Winchell, the famous newscaster, asking him to give the Jubilee some publicity. Letters were sent to all newspapers, asking them to tell their subscribers to listen to Winchell's news. On his national news broadcast he had this to say..."Cities and towns all over the country are now thinking about Father's and Mother's Days, and some have been suggesting a President's Day, however, it was Antioch, California that has gone them one better by having a week's celebration in honor of our President; calling it Antioch's Roosevelt Jubilee. It is to be held from April 18 to 23. More power, Antioch, OK Antioch!'

Antioch folks listening were thrilled as they seldom could be, to hear the most important broadcaster on the air take two minutes to tell the entire nation about their Jubilee. After Winchell's Sunday broadcast, other radio stations gave air time to the Antioch Roosevelt Jubilee among them was KGO, San Fransisco, and KGDM, Stockton.

The big celebration started small at a City Council meeting. The men were talking about the election of President Roosevelt. Bragdon R. Garrow, more familiarly known as "Brag" said he thought it would be a good idea if they sent aside a day for a celebration to show their confidence in the new president. In trying to decide what to call it they came up with President's Day, Back Roosevelt Day and finally someone suggested Roosevelt Jubilee. Before the meeting broke up that night, a tentative plan was made for a one day program on Saturday, April 15. After the townspeople found out about the plan it had grown to include Saturday and Sunday. Then it was found there were other important events taking place around that time. From all of this grew the plans for a week's celebration. Thus, Roosevelt Jubilee Week grew. "Brag" Garrow was made the general chairman because it was his idea.

The first item on the agenda was the Clean-up Week prior to the celebration. This included the entire town, divided into four sections, with section prizes for the best looking yard, new paint jobs for houses, barns, fences and out buildings, and a prize for vacant lots cleaned of trash and weeds. There was a prize for the block chairman whose block presented the best appearance. Two awards were given in the business district. Antioch never looked better and the Clean-up Week ended with a huge Bonfire Rally on Wednesday night, April 19.

This event was held downtown in the block bounded by 3rd and 4th Streets and E and F Streets. A stage was erected for the speakers and entertainers. When the flames from the big bonfire burned down, red flares were lighted and after they went out, the electric lights were turned on. The program included speeches, orchestra music. skits and the presentation of the prizes. The Clean-up Week was a tremendous success.

Dave Nelson was in charge of the Housing Committee which had the huge job of finding rooms for the participants and guests attending the Jubilee. All hotels and rooming houses were sold out for the week-long event.

The entire week was one big circus with carnival rides and concessions everywhere. Ferd Stamm was in charge of the Committee for the concessions

A large first aid station was established in the downtown area for medical emergencies.

The Police Department had at least 10 motorcycle officers under command of Al LeRoy to help with the traffic jams. The state motor patrolmen and several from the Sheriff's office were included in the 10 motorcycle officers. Judge John J. Brennan said he would try to be lenient with law breakers but warned that the Jubilee was not a special franchise for the commission of crimes. Chief of Police Stephens had the town well policed during the week, night and day with extra men in plain clothes.

Although the law was quite visible, many old-timers claim gambling was everywhere and the ladies of the night were in abundance.

A special stage show at the El Campanil Theater started off the Roosevelt Jubilee Week on Tuesday, April 18. The committee in charge of the event presented the week's program in revue form. "Brag" Garrow was presented with the key to the city and said the adopted slogan for the Jubilee was..." Something doing every minute."

The Theater had special shows all week with famous stars on stage and movies every day with special midnight shows. The radio station KGDM of Stockton had a special celebration opening broadcast on Tuesday evening.

The events held during the Jubilee were outstanding and probably will never be duplicated.

The East Contra Costa Rifle Club constructed a new firearm range on Wilbur Avenue With 15 targets. Eighteen different city teams took part in the biggest shoot ever held in this part of the state. Over 10.000 rounds of ammunition was ordered to supply the Jubilee shooters.

The Horseshoe Tournament received 40 entries from all over the state.

These were champion players, one who had pitched, in his last tournament, a total of 150 shoes with 127 ringers, the rest were doubles. Horseshoe pitching was a big event in those days. There were 16 courts for the event.

The Automobile Show was on lots on Third Street back of the ice plant. Several chassis exhibited at the San Fransisco Automobile Show was on display as well as the latest models of cars.

Almost all the downtown stores' display windows were decorated in historical themes for the merchants' Window Decoration Contest. The Fibreboard Company displayed the many products of their factories in one store window.

Official Jubilee hats were sold at the Palace Drug Store. They were special sailor hats in red, white and blue colors. The gobs' hat were chosen because Antioch was known as a city where water sports predominate.

An old fashioned auction was featured with a regular auctioneer. All sorts of articles were sold including a phonograph, electric motor, outboard motor, Fishing poles, automobile tires, bed room crockery (thunder pots), a horned toad, some livestock, books and many other things. Some fun was provided when 7 greased pigs were turned loose in the crowd. Whoever managed to hold onto the pigs kept them.

A special American Legion drum and bugle corps and drill team competition was held on Sunday. Posts from all over California entered the competition.

The Bicycle Races had over fifty riders registered with Babe Delulio who was in charge of the races. One race was run from Pittsburg to Antioch and four other races were run on Antioch streets. The Mayor's Challenge Race was a feature run with Mayor James Donlon, Fire Chief Ferd Stamm, Supervisor Richard Trembath, with two mysterious riders registered as "Handlebar Hank" and "Oakley Streak". The "Streak" was supposed to be a retired bicycle racer living in Oakley. The bicycles for this feature race were donated by the Oakland Cyclery.

Amos Stagg, the famous football coach, was honored at one of the many dinners held during the Jubilee. The Antioch Hospital had been renovated and entirely refinished so the hospital had an open house for the city's guests.

The merchants had their night at the El Campanil Theater on Friday where they made personal appearances at the mammoth show presented that night. Their acts were called, the Great Merchants All Star Vaudeville Show. Each group had prepared a vaudeville act and much fun was had. Also, there was the coronation of the Jubilee Queen who ruled over the celebration for the remainder of the week. The Queen was chosen during the contest for that honor by the number of votes received.

The Jubilee Ball on Saturday night packed the Veteran's Hall with dancers. There were special decorations and during the evening, the silver cup awards for the Saturday parade were presented with appropriate ceremony. The Ball was in honor of winning Queen who was crowned at the Friday night show at El Campanil Theater. Certificates of honor were given out for window displays. Dancing started at 8:45 PM.

The Air Circus and parachute jumps were featured both Saturday and Sunday. The Antioch Cranston Flying Field (for a fee) provided rides over the Diablo Valley by airplanes. Henry Cranston, owner, had induced a dozen well-known pilots to come to Antioch with their planes for the two days. One of the airplanes on exhibit was a cabin plane which gave the crowds an idea of what was used on cross-country flights.

The Antioch Boy Scouts presented a three ring circus in tents erected on the lots located at Third and G Streets. The circus performance lasted one hour. Pinkey LeRoy was the ring master. All the circus performers were scouts with their animals and pets. There was the usual side show with "unusual" freaks. A small fee was charged to help defray expenses for an hour packed with fun. It was a great show for children.

The big Pet Show, held on Saturday on the lots at Third and G streets, was a great success. Men, women and children exhibited their pets and show animals. There were dogs, cats, birds, horses and almost any type of pet, pedigree or otherwise. W. A. Noia, being in charge of the show, provided 25 cages and advised the exhibitors to bring their own cages. A lady with wide experience in judging animals at pet shows was the judge. The animals at the Show were judged on points of distinction and a first prize was awarded to the best of each species, also for the most interesting and unusual. Judging started at 11:00 AM right after the Saturday parade. Prizes were provided by the local merchants.

The Sixth Annual Antioch Flower Show was part of the celebration. The Flower Club's show was at the Legion Hall on April 20. Mrs. Grace Adams, who was in charge of their yearly show, said it was the largest in Contra Costa County and was due to the celebration. Twelve judges determined the winners of the many flower and garden entries.

The Roosevelt Jubilee Regatta on Sunday filled the waterfront with all types of yachts, motor boats and racing boats. The Regatta was sponsored by the Antioch Chamber of Commerce with the speedboat races being conducted under the auspices of the Northern California Outboard Association.

The Regatta brought out thousands of boat owners, crews, guests and out of town visitors. There were one hundred or more entries of speed boats from both amateur and professional drivers. The race course was one mile long. There was a patriotic dress parade of the yachts, motor boats and speed boats and then the program of racing began at 11:00 AM. A special reception committee of several Antioch girls served luncheon to the drivers at noon so there was no interruption in the races. The Sea Scouts from Martinez and Concord were there with their ships to render assistance needed in case of an emergency.

The speed boat races were so popular that outboard racing became a regular event on the Antioch waterfront for years. A local driver, Charles Benson, became National Outboard Champion.

A track meet was held during the Jubilee Week at Eells Field. There was, also, a tennis tournament and a bathing beauty contest as features on the Jubilee program.

The Jubilee Parade was the biggest and most brilliant spectacle ever seen in Antioch. It consisted of approximately 30 decorated floats, with drum corps, marching bands, drill teams, decorated automobiles, mounted horses, Antioch fire trucks, clowns etc. There were more than 1700 persons who participated in the Jubilee Parade which was held on Saturday at 1:30 PM. Silver cups were awarded to best contestants in their parade divisions. Cranston's Air Circus airplanes flew over the marching route and performed aerial antics during the parade.

A second parade, The American Legion Parade, was held on Sunday. It was sponsored by Posts from all over California. This parade started at 10:00 AM and many of the participants were the same as the Jubilee Parade. It was almost as big and lavish as Saturday's parade.

A motion picture company made movies of the events on Saturday and Sunday for the El Campanil Theater.

The Antioch Roosevelt Jubilee Week ended Sunday, April 23, 1933 and the city will never see another celebration as big or exciting as this one.

March 31, 1933.
DEAR MR. WINCHELL:

At a meeting on March 6, 1933, just 48 hours after the inauguration of our splendid new President, Mr. F. D. Roosevelt, Antioch's live wires decided that Antioch should be the first city in the nation to stage a Roosevelt Jubilee.

The results are enclosed. We're a very small town and maybe you have never heard of us but we've got a "Big Idea."

We are looking for publicity and Walter Winchell can give it to us.

I am going to shoot the news to every paper in this county, asking the radio listeners to tune in on your program with the idea that they "might" hear something about the "Antioch Roosevelt Jubilee."

We don't care what you say about us but say something. Give a small town with a "Big Idea" a break. We will all be waiting 'round our radios next Sunday.

O. K. Walter Winchell,
Hoping you do. Yours truly,
GENERAL CHAIRMAN OF
ROOSEVELT JUBILEE.
BRG : VB.

Jubilee for Roosevelt Is Heralded to Whole Nation

PROCLAMATION

WHEREAS, Antioch will on Saturday, April 22, participate in and witness, the first and greatest parade demonstration, in connection with Antioch's Roosevelt Jubilee; and,

WHEREAS, there will be many visitors here for the occasion, to pay tribute to our President; and,

WHEREAS, a festival and holiday spirit will prevail;

NOW, THEREFORE, I, JAS. D. DONLON, Mayor of Antioch, do hereby proclaim that it is fitting and due that proper recognition be given the occasion by the people of Antioch; that all take part; that our visitors be made welcome; that we demonstrate our sincerity of purpose.

THEREFORE, it is requested that to fittingly express our loyalty and support, all business houses close on Saturday afternoon, April 22, from the hours of 1:30 to 3:30, while the Jubilee Parade is in progress.

JAS. D. DONLON,
Mayor of the City of Antioch.

April 17, 1933.

"President Roosevelt signing the Roosevelt Jubilee of Antioch, Calif. for Brag Garrow"
Inscription on back of original 1933 photograph. No identification of other people.
Courtesy Admiral Jack A. Garrow

287

El Campanil Theater Decorated for the Roosevelt Jubilee.
Roosevelt's portrait above marquee. From Stamm Collection

Speed boat with outboard motor, one of the class of
racers used in the Roosevelt Jubilee River Races.
From Author's Collection

(L. to R.) Brag Garrow Jr., Layne Garrow, Jack Garrow and Brag Garrow, Jubilee Chairman. Wedding day of Jack and Layne, June 3, 1955, Annapolis, MD.

Courtesy Admiral Jack Garrow

Theater Float with Jubilee Queen, Attendants and Musicians.
From Stamm Collection